A Trifle, A Coddle, A Fry

GEORGE BERNARD SHAW • JAMES JOYCE • MARY LAVIN

SOMERVILLE & ROSS • OLIVER ST JOHN GOGARTY

ELIZABETH BOWEN • SAMUEL BECKETT • MOLLY KEANE

PATRICK KAVANAGH • SEÁN O'CASEY • KATE O'BRIEN • GEORGE MOORE

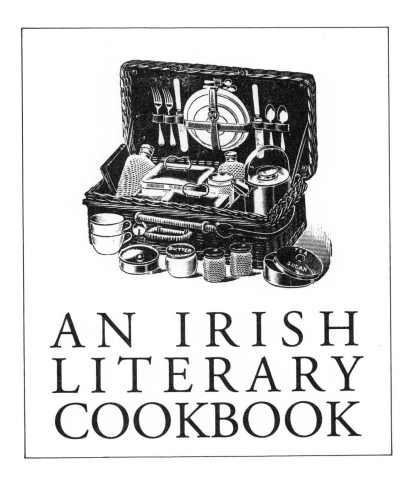

AN IRISH LITERARY COOKBOOK

VERONICA JANE O'MARA & FIONNUALA O'REILLY

Moyer Bell
Wakefield, Rhode Island & London

Published by Moyer Bell

First published by Town House and Country House, 1991, 42 Morehampton Road, Donnybrook, Dublin 4, Ireland

---

**Library of Congress
Cataloging-in-Publication Data**

O'Mara, Veronica Jane
   [Cooking the books]
   A trifle, a coddle, a fry : an Irish literary cookbook / Veronica
Jane O'Mara, Fionnuala O'Reilly.
     p.   cm.
   First published in 1991 under title: Cooking the books.
   ISBN 1-55921-081-8
   1. Cookery, Irish. 2. Literary cookbooks. I. O'Reilly,
Fionnuala. II. Title.
TX717.5.O46   1993
641.59415—dc20   92-37713
                                       CIP

Printed in the United States of America

We dedicate this book to our two families and thank them for their appetites.

Contents

List of Recipes

ACKNOWLEDGEMENTS

The authors and publishers would like to thank the following for permission to quote copyright material:

Faber and Faber Ltd, London, for short quotations from *The Selected Letters of Somerville and Ross*, ed. by Gifford Lewis; The Curtis Brown Group Ltd, on behalf of the Executors of Sir Patrick Coghill Bt, for extracts from *In the Vine Country* and *Some Irish Yesterdays*, copyright E OE Somerville and Martin Ross; Virago Press, London, for extracts from *Through Connemara in a Governess Cart* by Somerville and Ross; Chatto & Windus, London, and the estates of the authors for extracts from *The Real Charlotte* by Somerville and Ross; MacDonald & Co, London, for extracts from *Some Experiences of an Irish RM* and *Further Experiences of an Irish RM* by Somerville and Ross; Grove Press, Inc., New York, for extracts from *Endgame, Whoroscope, Murphy, More Pricks Than Kicks, Molloy, Malone Dies, Krapp's Last Tape* and *How It Is* by Samuel Beckett; Victor Gollancz Ltd for extracts from *The Life of George Moore* by Joseph Hone; Alfred A. Knopf Inc., New York, for extracts from *Time After Time* and *Good Behaviour* by Molly Keane; Dutton, an imprint of New American Library, a division of Penguin Books USA, Inc. for extracts from *Queen Lear*; Viking Penguin, a division of Penguin Books USA Inc. for 'various excerpts' from *Dubliners* by James Joyce, copyright 1916 by B W Heubsch, definitive text copyright 1967 by the Estate of James Joyce, and for extracts from *Finnegans Wake* by James Joyce, copyright 1939 by James Joyce, copyright renewed 1967 by George Joyce and Lucia Joyce; The Society of Authors on behalf of the Bernard Shaw Estate for extracts from *Heartbreak House, Getting Married, John Bull's Other Island, The Philanderer, The Intelligent Woman's Guide to Socialism . . .* , *A Village Wooing, You Never Can Tell* and various articles and letters; Macmillan London Ltd and Eileen O'Casey for extracts from Seán O'Casey's *Autobiographies* and *Juno and the Paycock*; David Higham Associates Ltd, London, for extracts from *Without My Cloak, The Last of Summer, As Music and Splendour, The Flower of May* and *Pray for the Wanderer* by Kate O'Brien, originally published by Heinemann Ltd, London, and from *My Ireland* by Kate O'Brien, originally published by B T Batsford Ltd, London; the trustees of the Estate of Patrick Kavanagh, % Peter Fallon, Literary Agent, Loughcrew, Oldcastle, Co. Meath, for quotations from the writings of Patrick Kavanagh; Mary Lavin for extracts from *In the Middle of the Fields, Tales from Bective Bridge, The House in Clewe Street, A Family Likeness, A Memory and Other Stories* and *The Patriot Sun*

We would like to thank the following for the photographs:
   G A Duncan, Dublin, for 'Kate O'Brien' and 'Patrick Kavanagh'; The Curtis Brown Group Ltd for 'Elizabeth Bowen'; John Minihane, Evening Standard, for 'Samuel Beckett'; Elliott & Fry Ltd for 'Seán O'Casey'; Clare Williams for 'Oliver St John Gogarty'; Ted McCarthy, Irish Times, for 'Mary Lavin'; Colin Smythe, Gerrards Cross, Buckinghamshire, for 'G B Shaw' and 'George Moore'; André Deutsch for 'Somerville and Ross'; Beinecke Library, Yale University, for 'James Joyce'.
   Special thanks to Molly Keane, Mary Lavin, Oliver Duane Gogarty, Eileen O'Casey, John O'Riordain, James O'Reilly, J Patrick Duffner, Kevin Myers, Anya Corless, Colin Smyth, Orla Clarke, Frances Laffan, Biddy White-Lennon, Dennis Latimer and Muireann Noonan.
   Every effort has been made to trace copyright holders. The Publishers apologise for any error or omissions in the above list and would be grateful to be notified of any corrections that should be incorporated in the next edition of this volume.

The Authors

Veronica Jane O'Mara was educated at University College Dublin and Trinity College Dublin. She has worked in the theatre and in education and is now a researcher for film and television. She has an abiding love for second-hand bookshops, puns and rather long lunches. Veronica is married with three children and lives by the sea in County Dublin.

Fionnuala O'Reilly was educated at University College Dublin and has worked in the rag trade and in the antiques business. A Dubliner, with a passion for food and gardening, her collection of Victorian and Edwardian cookery books is the source of her culinary inspiration, and her gardening is in the tradition of that remarkable Irishwoman, Norah Lindsay.

Introduction

A summer or so ago we met a Japanese gentleman at a Dublin dinner party, who fell in through the door, rather the worse for wear, after a literary pub crawl. Fionn suggested that a literary food crawl would be less incapacitating, and Veronica idly surmised that such a tour could form the basis for a book. And so the idea of 'cooking' Irish literature was conceived.

As our favourite things in life are food and books (Fionn), and books and food (Veronica), we felt we were fairly well suited to the task of tracking down the heroic culinary episodes of our writers. Like literary magpies of the best sort, we chose what amused us, emulating Somerville and Ross; 'We went where we would and did what pleased us most.'

So, despite the fact that W B Yeats commended his wife George on their home-grown horseradish sauce, that J M Synge lived on dried ling and potatoes on the Aran Islands, and that Lady Augusta Gregory masterminded the jam-making at Coole Park like Caesar and the invasion of Gaul, they only receive honourable mentions. However, we do regret Brendan Behan's bath of Irish stew, in which sheeps' heads, chickens and the unidentifiable bobbed about in apparent felicity.

Despite the addition of more than a few pounds to our collective body weight, the inevitable consequences of eating our way through the Anglo-Irish canon, we have no regrets about following James Joyce's suggestion to be speakable about eatables; so 'change the plates for the next course of Murphies!'

1

George Moore

George Moore, author, art critic and bon viveur, with a taste for the outrageous, was born at Moore Hall in County Mayo. He had hoped to be an artist but instead turned to writing, believing his talents as an artist to be insufficient. His reputation as an important novelist was assured by *Esther Waters* in 1894. In 1901 he moved to Dublin to assist Yeats, Martyn, Synge and Lady Gregory at the birth of the Irish Literary Theatre. *The Untilled Field* and *The Lake* were the fruits of the Irish experience. A clash of personalities led him to return to London, but his view of that extraordinary time is recorded with customary malice and incorrigible tactlessness in three volumes of his autobiography, *Hail and Farewell.* He wrote more than a dozen novels, and claimed that women were the mainspring of his inspiration. George Moore died in London.

George Moore　　　1852 to 1933

> I was a long time before I could do a French omelette to suit him;
> in the end he had to go to a small hotel in Buckingham Palace
> Road, to ask the French chef to show me. After I had seen it
> done, I soon got to do it all right for him. Very often he would
> crave a fish that was not in season.
>
> *(Mrs Clara Warville, George Moore's cook and housekeeper 1920-33,*
> *describing her employer in Joseph Hone's biography.)*

Well might Mrs Clara Warville pay careful attention to the omelette-making lessons, for all Dublin knew that when George Moore lived at number 4 Ely Place, he had treated his cook to a dose of rough justice for serving a sub-standard omelette. Oliver St John Gogarty describes the scene:

He sat at the head of an oval table with his back to the garden and the street. In the quiet cul-de-sac nothing stirred; neither vehicles nor foot passengers entered Ely Place after sundown. The soup passed scrutiny. Moore was acting as a gourmet of the most exquisite taste before his guests. He had been in France and we were paying for it.

'It is impossible to convince a cook that she should heat the tureen before pouring in the soup. In these old houses the stairs to the kitchen are enough to cool the soup. The real test of a cook, however, is the omelette. Now we shall see.'...

He lifted the lid of the chafing dish. He replaced it with an exclamation. He went hurriedly into his hall, opened the hall door and blew a police whistle. He returned with a young constable whose helmet was held respectfully under his arm. Moore again raised the lid of the dish and, pointing to the omelette, said, 'Look at that!' While the lid was coming off, the constable's helmet was being put on. The constable gazed at the omelette, looked at us all, and then at the omelette. Moore said, 'I want you to arrest the perpetrator of that atrocity.' The young policeman stood bewildered.

The constable at last spoke: 'On what charge, sir?' For a moment Moore was nonplussed. Then he rallied and, lifting the lid, pointed with it. 'That is no omelette. Go down and arrest her for obtaining money under false pretences.'

George Moore (known as GM to his friends) took food very, very seriously indeed; add to the subject of food, paintings (he 'discovered' Manet), writing and women, and you have the man; arbiter and epicure, gossip and trouble-maker.

GM was incorrigibly indiscreet and loved to shock his audience (a delight dating from his Mayo childhood when he used to take off his clothes and run away from his horrified nurse). Malice and wit were common currency in the literary Dublin of those days; what is endearing about Moore is that he practised the art of detraction, not only orally but he wrote it down too. *Hail and Farewell* is a precious mine of gossip and scandal.

Sir Thornley Stoker, the surgeon and Bram Stoker's brother, was one of Moore's neighbours in Ely Place. He gave a dinner one night which featured a fine salmon, of which he was rather proud.

Sir Thornley asked: 'The shoulder or the belly of this salmon, Moore? I'm chining the salmon. I killed this fish in the Slaney — King Harman's water — and I think we'll find it a palatable fish. Shall I help you to the shoulder?'
'No, I think the fin, Sir Thornley.'
'Now, Moore, don't be peevish. You are the last that should pretend to be careless about food. I've just been reading your long letter to The Irish Times *on the grey mullet. Nobody ever heard of a fin.'*
'On the contrary, the Chineses — as my friend here insists on calling them — find shark's fin delicious.'

Shortly after this interchange the diningroom door opens and Lady Stoker runs in, naked and insane. After her recapture, Sir Thornley begs discretion of his guests, but Moore cannot resist a comment, 'But it was charming, Sir Thornley, I demand an encore'.

Moore simply was incapable of resisting the risqué comment, the off-colour story, the salacious piece of gossip, especially in mixed company. After coming from an assignation with his mistress he said to Yeats, 'I do wish that woman would wash!' When told about an illicit couple who had gone to bed together, he asked, 'And did their hands stray?' Before he travelled to Palestine to research *The Brook Kerith* he said he was going to order 'camels and concubines — 50 of one and 300 of the other'. He didn't believe there was a decent hotel in Dublin, and although he always stayed at the Shelbourne in St Stephen's Green, he wrote:

> *The meals in the Shelbourne Hotel*
> *Make one wish one were dead and in hell.*

And in the marvellous novel *Drama in Muslin,* the dinner at the Shelbourne culminates in a decidedly nasty dessert of a 'few dried oranges and tough grapes'. No wonder Edward Martyn called him 'a bit of a bank holiday sort of fellow'.

Edward Martyn lived in Tullyra Castle in County Galway, a neighbour of Lady Gregory's. If GM was a gourmet, then Edward was a gourmand; he was also a misogynist and a fanatical Catholic. GM was slightly built, with champagne-bottle shoulders, and 'dear Edward' was positively obese — they made an unlikely pair. In *As I was Going Down Sackville Street* Gogarty describes Martyn, not without malice:

> *But soon it will be eight o'clock and he will scent the beef at the Kildare Street Club. He will seize his stick and his man will help his protein-crippled limbs to the carnivorous festival of rheumatism and gout.*

However, the Friday that Moore goes to Tullyra Castle for dinner, and discovers that the salmon has not arrived from Galway, he is offered a very different menu:

> *If there had been a slice of Double Gloucester in the larder of Tullyra, I should not have minded the absence of the salmon. But to be told I must dine off two eggs and a potato, so that his conscience should not be troubled during the night, worried me, and I am afraid I cast many an angry look across the table. An apple pie came up and some custards, and these soothed me; he discovered some marmalade in a cupboard, and Edward is such a sociable being when his pipe is alight, that I forgave his theological prejudices for the sake of his aesthetic.*

Moore's favourite subject was himself, in particular himself in love, and he was so insistent about informing everyone of his affairs that his veracity was questioned. Susan Mitchell, poet and assistant editor to AE (George Russell, the mystic poet and visionary philosopher) on the newspaper *The*

Irish Homestead, did not believe him; 'Some men kiss and do not tell, some kiss and tell; but George Moore tells and does not kiss.' Sadly, we cannot really include AE in a literary cookbook for he existed somewhere on an astral plain, far removed from the rest of us mere materialists, although a recipe for faerie cakes might be appropriate.

By 1908, disillusionment had jaundiced Moore's Irish vision of 'poets and painters burgeoning on every bush', and he wrote to Eduoard Dujardin, 'The Celtic Renaissance does not exist, it is a myth.' He decided to return to London. Susan Mitchell composed an ode of farewell:

> *My naughty problematic past was nothing but a sham;*
> *My sins and my repentance all paper and all cram.*
> *Some day you'll all discover how respectable I am,*
> *Revere the marriage state, believe in Abraham.*
> *And for Gaels and their revivals don't really care a damn.*

In his work George Moore's constant theme is love and passion; his inspiration — women.

The diet his characters follow is a rather plain and stodgy bourgeois one; a plethora of cutlets and chickens and roasts, and no cheese. George Moore loved cheese, especially Double Gloucester, and felt that the absence of cheese-making in Ireland betokened a certain lack of civilisation. 'We are not great cheese eaters in Ireland' says Mrs Grattan in the short story 'The Wild Goose'; she is an execrable cook who roasts on Sundays and Thursdays, turning the leftovers into a succession of hash, mince and shepherd's pie. In 'A Letter to Rome', the priest believes he has solved the problem of emigration, the haemorrhage that in the 1880s was leaving the entire countryside empty and desolate. 'If each priest were to take a wife about 4000 children would be born within the year', and they would be fine and healthy, for the priests lived in the best homes and ate the best food. Wedding feasts are described; pig's head, sheeps' tongues and a barrel of porter. Brawn and cabbage simmers odoriferously and griddle cakes and strawberries make a fine breakfast. In 'Esther Waters', life below stairs in England is exposed. The same stodgy diet pertains as in Ireland, the remains from the diningroom become the meal for the servants: mutton, beefsteak pudding, curry, with blancmange and jelly and currant tart for dessert.

Nancy Cunard in her memoir of Moore describes a typical dinner at 121 Ebury Street, SWI: 'a delicious *bisque*, a perfectly timed omelette, a pheasant for GM to fuss over and a delectable milky baby-pudding'. Her mother, Maud, known as 'the pocket Venus', was perhaps Moore's most enduring companion, their relationship surviving her marriage and countless arguments; his temper being as erratic as his spelling. Nancy Cunard writes of his rich wonderful voice, 'a bubbling hot dish of a voice', dough-like hands and characteristic laugh 'Khk, Khk, Khk!'. Susan Mitchell immortalised Moore's gastronomic reputation in her poem 'George Moore Eats a Grey Mullet':

I sailed away from France, alas!
My heart was wildly grieving,
For all a man of taste was gas-
Tronomically leaving.
No woman from my heart I tore-
The sex will always find me-
I fretted for no girl, but for
A fish I'd left behind me.

The cooks of France, how great they be,
And of their art how willing,
And in thy restaurant, Henri,
I had spent many a shilling.
When on my plate that wondrous day,
Le Bar, I first did find thee,
O France! why did I sail away
And leave thy fish behind me?

I've sought it over London town
And eke in Dublin city,
At many a table I've sat down,
Nor found it, more's the pity.
O Irish maids, with eyes so meek,
Should ardent glances blind ye,
Mine eyes seek not your hearts, they seek
A fish I left behind me.

BASS À LA SAUCE IRLANDAISE

Mr Moore was very fond of a fish called bass, which he could never get at any of the small fish shops, so he asked me to go to the Army and Navy Stores, and ask if they ever had bass to sell. They said yes they did have it sometimes but no one seemed to ask for it. True, it was a very nice-flavoured fish, and was nice even when cold with mayonnaise sauce. Mr Moore said it was eaten a great deal in France.

Mrs Clara Warville

Our desire was to serve our bass with a cardinal sauce so that we could tell you all about George Moore's ferocious anti-clericalism and how he exposed the extraordinary power that lay in the hands of the Catholic clergy in the 1880s. Priests are portrayed as ruling their impoverished parishes with a blind inhumanity; kings in an empty landscape. Do read *The Untilled Field* — it's a delight. Back to the sauce. Lobster is a lot dearer today than when George Moore walked this earth, so we suggest a patriotic alternative. The striking colour of this delectable mayonnaise will remind you instead of Moore's green period.

Bass should be cooked the same way as salmon, either poached in a court bouillon, as below, or if you prefer, baked in the oven at 180°C (350°F, Gas mark 4) for 20 minutes per lb.

> 1 sea bass (about 1kg/2lb)
> 2 pt (1l) of water
> 1 tsp salt
> 1 bouquet garni (1 bayleaf, a sprig each of parsley, thyme, fennel and marjoram)
> 2 onions, chopped
> 2 carrots, chopped
> 2 tbsp (60ml) vinegar
> marjoram

If you have any leftover white wine, it is a good addition, either with or instead of the water. Simmer all the ingredients except the fish for 30 minutes, then strain and use to poach the fish. About 15 minutes to the pound is generally long enough, but if your fish weighs more than 7lb, you should allow 20 to 25 minutes per lb. Serves four.

Sauce Irlandaise

This is a green mayonnaise with green vegetables chopped into it.

> 2 eggs
> 2 tbsp tarragon vinegar
> pinch of salt
> lots of pepper
> 2 pt (1l) olive oil
> chives
> parsley
> scallions (spring onions)

Put the eggs and vinegar in a food processor. Season well and beat till frothy. Then, with the machine at full speed, start pouring in the oil in a slow trickle. If it gets too thick, add a tablespoon or two of warm water. To make the mayonnaise green, add a handful each of chives and parsley and some green ends of scallions (spring onions), all chopped very finely. To this green mayonnaise add cold cooked vegetables; peas, broad beans, asparagus tips and broccoli all go very well with it. Allow about 2lb (1kg) of green vegetables for 2 pt (1l) of mayonnaise. Serves four.

POT-AU-FEU

The night he arrived home I gave him one of his favourite soups, a French soup called *pot au feu*, also some fried filleted sole with hollandaise sauce. He did not want any sweet, but said after dinner that I saved his life. I did not understand what he meant by that, so I said, 'In what way?' and he said 'By giving me something that I could eat'.

Mrs Clara Warville

George Moore's cook considered *pot-au-feu* as an adequate soup course, but this wholesome and filling dish deserves the title of a main course for the eating habits of today. It is quick and easy to make; our children like it, so it is to be recommended for family dinners on cold winter nights.

2lb (1kg) leg beef, chopped
1 tsp (5ml) salt
10 peppercorns, crushed
1 onion
bouquet garni
2 cloves garlic, chopped
2 carrots, peeled and sliced
2 celery stalks, chopped
1lb (480g) potatoes, peeled and halved
chopped fresh parsley to garnish

Put the meat in a heavy pot, cover with water, add the salt and bring to the boil slowly. Skim, then lower the heat, add the pepper, onion, bouquet garni and garlic. Cover the pot and simmer gently for 2¹/₂ hours. Add the vegetables and simmer for another hour, till the vegetables are tender. Skim to remove any fat and serve with a sprinkling of parsley.
Serves six.

ELIZABETH O'REGAN'S APPLE RICE

It seemed to him that Catherine would never leave off handing round something. Just now it was potatoes, now it was greens; and he watched Scanlan and Maloney, and thought of what they had already eaten: their share of the cod-fish, four large chops, and now they were holding out their plates and receiving wings and legs. The fowls were followed by a pie made of rice and eggs, and when it was finished Catherine brought in a dish of stewed apples and custard.

The Lake, *revised edition of 1905 and omitted from the revised edition of 1921*

The priests in George Moore's works always seem to eat the best food, and Father Gogarty's dinner party sounds delicious. There is a character in *The Lake* called 'the detestable Mrs O'Mara' who has a beguiling tongue and the appearance of a midwife. There was no discussion about who claimed this recipe. Mere mention of rice, eggs and stewed apple has the unfortunate effect of causing Veronica to drool, as her Aunty Mary used to make her this dessert when she first came to Dublin. She actually prefers it to posh French puds, so forget the vacherin and peel the apples! Aunty Mary got the recipe from her mother, an independent lady and one of the first Irish women to go to university at the turn of the century. Her home in Dun Laoghaire was one of Michael Collins's network of safe houses.

4 cooking apples
3oz (90g) sugar
1 pt (600ml) milk
1 1/2oz (45g) ground rice
1oz (30g) sugar
2 eggwhites
lemon rind
1/2oz (15g) butter, cut into small pieces

Preheat oven to 150°C (300°F, Gas mark 2).

Peel and chop the apples. Stew with 2oz sugar and a little water until soft. Heat the milk until boiling. Remove from the heat and sprinkle the ground rice onto the milk and stir. Return to the stove, simmer and stir until thick and creamy. Remove from the stove and sprinkle with 1oz sugar. Beat the eggwhites and lemon rind until stiff. Fold into the rice mixture. Put the stewed apple in an ovenproof dish. Spoon the rice mixture on top. Dot with butter and sprinkle on some castor sugar. Bake for 45 minutes until the top is golden.
Serves four.

OMELETTE SOUFFLÉE

And similar wise sayings were often scattered through Mrs
Barton's conversation, for she knew well, although her chatter was
always *en omelette soufflée*, a little seasoning thought would not
come amiss, even to the lightest appetite.

A Drama in Muslin

A sweet omelette is something of an *avis rara* on today's menus. It is rather an
unusual dessert to serve but is easy to make and, like the parfait, can be varied using
different fruit, jams and liqueurs. We have to say that neither of us would have
possessed the brass neck to cook an omelette for dear old GM.

Omelette Soufflée

> 2 eggs
> 1oz (30g) castor sugar
> 2 drops of vanilla essence
> 1 pinch grated lemon rind

Preheat the oven to 200°C (400°F, Gas mark 6).

Separate the eggs. Beat the yolks with the sugar, vanilla and lemon rind until a pale
froth. Beat the whites till stiff; fold in the yolks. Pour into a well-buttered soufflé
dish and bake for 12 minutes. Serve at once with whipped cream and a sauce of
apricot jam melted with some rum or brandy. A variation of this omelette is to put
fruit in the bottom of the dish; blackberries are particularly good.
Serves one.

Sweet Omelette

> 2 eggs
> grated rind and juice of one lemon
> 1 tbsp cream
> 1 dessertspoon sugar
> butter to fry
> apricot jam

Preheat the pan and turn on the grill. Separate the eggs. Beat the yolks with the lemon rind, juice, cream and sugar until a pale froth. Beat the whites until stiff and fold into the yolks.

Cook the omelette on a hot pan on which the butter is sizzling. Lower the temperature gradually while cooking. Cook for about 5 to 8 minutes. Hold the pan under the hot grill for a few minutes to cook the top of the omelette. Put the jam in the centre and fold over. Turn out onto a plate and sprinkle with castor sugar. Serve with whipped cream and jam to which a little rum has been added.
Serves one.

PARFAIT À LA TURQUE

Sir Owen Asher said, 'There is a parfait — that comes before the soufflé of course.'

Evelyn Innes

Fionn thinks this a perfect dessert because the ways of changing the flavours are endless, just add whatever you like...

> 4 egg yolks
> 4oz (120g) caster sugar
> $\frac{1}{2}$ cup very strong coffee (2 full tsp of instant coffee in a $\frac{1}{2}$ cup of water)
> $\frac{3}{4}$ pt (450ml) cream
> 2 tbsp (60ml) brandy
> 4 eggwhites

Beat the egg yolks with the sugar to a pale froth. Add the coffee and $\frac{1}{2}$ pt (300 ml) cream. Pour into a heavy saucepan and stir over a low heat until the custard coats the back of a spoon. Cool completely and chill. Beat the remaining cream and add the brandy. Chill.

Whip the eggwhites until stiff. Add the brandied cream to the custard, then fold in the eggwhites. Freeze in a metal container if possible. This is a very adaptable recipe; simply change the flavour of the custard. For *Parfait à la Japonais*, omit the coffee and add 4oz (120g) of toasted brown bread crumbs and half a wine glass of strong sherry to the custard; change the brandy in the cream for any liqueur you fancy.

Serves six.

CROSS TREACLE PUDDING

'The Cronins do not eat soup,' he said, 'but they are addicted to
apple pies, custards, and treacle pudding.'

The Untilled Field

In the story *The Wild Goose*, Mr Cronin and his daughter become rather cross
about who should have the last slice of treacle pudding, so take care this doesn't
happen in your house. Mealtimes can be fraught occasions in the most well-ordered
establishments, but a row over treacle pudding might be deemed excessive.
Veronica has a clinging memory of school steamed pudding which stuck to the roof
of the mouth — this pud is not at all like that, but is light and mouth-watering.

    4oz (120g) plain flour
    2oz (60g) soft brown sugar
    4oz (120g) shredded suet
    4oz (120g) fresh white breadcrumbs
    pinch of salt
    1 tsp bicarbonate of soda
    1 tsp ground ginger
    3 tbsp blackstrap molasses
    4 tbsp golden syrup
    1 egg, beaten
    1 tbsp milk

Mix all the dry ingredients together. Warm the molasses and 2 tablespoons of the
golden syrup. Mix them into the dry ingredients. Add the egg and the milk. Grease
a 1½ pt pudding basin very well and put in the remaining 2 tbsp of golden syrup.
Then add the pudding mixture. Cover with 2 thicknesses of greaseproof paper.
Make a pleat in the centre of the paper and tie well with string. Steam for 1½ to
2 hours; serve with custard. A spaghetti pot makes a very useful steamer for
pudding.

Treacle pudding is delicious, with a rich flavour of molasses and ginger. If you
want a blander pudding, try Treacle Sponge below, which has no molasses in it.
Serves six.

Treacle Sponge

> 4oz (120g) margarine or butter
> 4oz (120g) castor sugar
> 2 Size 1 eggs
> 4oz (120g) self-raising flour
> 4 tbsp golden syrup

Cream the butter and sugar. Add the eggs and flour and beat well. Grease a $1\frac{1}{2}$ to 2 pint pudding basin well; spoon in the golden syrup, then the sponge mixture. Cover with 2 thicknesses of greaseproof paper; make a pleat in the centre of the paper. Tie well with string and steam for $1\frac{1}{2}$ to 2 hours. Serve with custard. Serves six.

2

George Bernard Shaw

George Bernard Shaw, playwright, critic and universal savant was born in Dublin, where he lived impecuniously and unloved. He moved to London and wrote unsuccessful novels until his work as music critic on *The Star* established his literary reputation. His first play, *Widowers' Houses*, was produced in 1892, followed by *The Philanderer, Mrs Warren's Profession, Arms and the Man, Candida* and *You Never Can Tell.* None of these were successful, but fame arrived with the acclaimed *The Devil's Disciple* in New York in 1897. Harley Granville Barker's gifted productions of Shaw's plays at the Royal Court Theatre assured his reputation in London. Shaw considered *Heartbreak House* his best play, but the popular vote would probably go to *St Joan* and *Pygmalion.* Shaw expressed opinions on every possible subject and held forth entertainingly and courageously on soap boxes, in books and in the prefaces of the plays. He was an ardent socialist. He was awarded the Nobel Prize in 1925. Shaw died in Ayot St Lawrence in Hertfordshire.

George Bernard Shaw 1856 to 1950

There are millions of vegetarians in the world, but only one Bernard Shaw. A century ago there were millions of vegetarians and only one Shelley. Twenty-six centuries ago there were millions of them and only one Pythagoras. You do not obtain eminence quite so cheaply as by eating macaroni instead of mutton chops.

'Life Without Meat', *The Daily Chronicle*, 1 March 1918

Bernard Shaw was no gourmet — he thought eating was as unimportant an experience as dressing and undressing — but he wrote and spoke on the subject of his diet with the energy, style and humour that we expect from the 'pantomime ostrich'. Shaw became converted to vegetarianism at the beginning of 1881 while living at his mother's house in Fitzroy Square in London. His mother made no concessions to his change of diet and so he took pot luck with the soup and whatever vegetables came with the main course. His days were spent at the British Museum, his 'university', where he read voraciously and later wrote the novels which were not to make him famous. In the surrounding area there sprang up a clutch of vegetarian restaurants, which enabled him to eat very cheaply, basking in their 'pure air'.

Poverty was a constant element in those early London years, 'years of unbroken failure and rebuff with crises of broken boots and desperate clothes'. His mother's disinterest in his well-being caused him no surprise however as she had maintained an attitude of neutral unconcern since his birth. Many years later he wrote to Ellen Terry of his 'devil of a childhood...rich only in dreams, frightful and loveless in realities.' Neither loved nor hated, the little boy lived in an emotional vacuum. The lonely, neglected child ate in the kitchen with the servants:

stewed beef, which I loathed, badly cooked potatoes, sound or diseased as the case may be and much too much tea out of a brown delft teapot left to 'draw' on the hob until it was pure tannin. Sugar I stole...

When his mother, a fine mezzo-soprano, became involved with Vandeleur Lee, later following him to London, it was Shaw's chance to escape Dublin, a 'city of derision', and begin the proper Shavian career in London. He became a Fabian socialist, an orator and a music critic, and he made friends and joined the cycling craze that hit Victorian England. 'Yes, bicycling's a capital thing for a literary man', and so were visits to the little places that sprouted up all over the countryside, offering teas for cyclists. Shaw reckoned that, to become a champion cyclist, the ideal diet was brown bread and blackcurrant jam.

Unashamedly didactic, irresistibly funny, Shaw loves to stand our experience of life on its head; things are rarely what they seem in his plays, and jokes can be discovered in the strangest places. Heroes are anti-heroes, climax becomes anti-climax, and endings are often surprising. Shaw said his plays were all masterpieces and all talk. And while they talk, his characters drink a lot of tea, and even consume non-vegetarian meals in between the lines.

In *Widowers' Houses*, it almost seems as if Shaw uses tea and meals to punctuate the action as Blanche and Harry experience unexpected reversals in their betrothal plans.

Heartbreak House begins with tea for Ellie Dunn, which seems an ordinary enough event until Captain Shotover chucks it into a leather bucket and insists on making her his own special tea: 'Now before high heaven they have given this innocent child India tea — the stuff they tan their own leather insides with.... You shall have some of my tea. Do not touch that fly-blown cake: nobody eats it here except the dogs.'

Tea is also served within minutes of the opening of *Mrs Warren's Profession*. The redoubtable Mrs Warren, a highly successful owner-manager of a string of bordellos, calls in her guests for tea with the warning that, if they don't hurry up, the teacake will be cold. Later in the play, her daughter serves a supper of cold beef, lettuce and cheese, which does not please Mrs Warren's delicate palate.

The invalid diet of beans and soda water imposed on the liverish Craven is called into question in *The Philanderer*, when Dr Padmore discovers that he has made a mistake and his patient is not ill at all. Craven's daughters, both 'advanced women' and members of the Ibsen Club, immediately enjoin him to accompany them for a beefsteak in the club diningroom. Dr Padmore still hopes to marry Julia, one of the daughters, and invites her to tea. Act III begins with the nervous doctor ensconced behind the kettle and the teapot.

Padmore:	*There! Making tea is one of the few things I consider myself able to do thoroughly well. Cake?*
Julia:	*No, thank you. I don't like sweet things.*

But she does agree to marriage!

In *John Bull's Other Island* a jokey look is taken at that most unamusing of subjects — the relations between England and Ireland. The serving of food in this play seems far more than a dramatic convention, for it illustrates the Irish way of life for the Englishman Broadbent. His first impression of Roscullen is of an 'Irishness' that he finds irresistibly charming. Poor Patsy 'the butter-fingered omadhaun' is the traditional Irish eejit (a word in the Hiberno-English dialect denoting idiot, as in Dostoevsky). In attempting to carry the luggage of three men, a hamper, a goose and a salmon, he naturally lets some of it go:

Cornelius:	*Oh, be the hokey, the sammin's broke in two! You shtoopid ass, what d'ye mean?*
Father Dempsey:	*Are you drunk, Patsy Farrell? Did I tell you to carry that hamper carefully or did I not?*
Patsy:	*[rubbing the back of his head, which has almost dinted a slab of granite] Sure me fut slipt. Howkn I carry three men's luggage at wanst?*

Broadbent feels disappointed when Aunt Julia tells him he's in time for tea, because he assumes she means a cup of tea and that there's no dinner. In the Irish countryside, dinner is eaten in the middle of the day, and tea means supper. Interestingly, the tea Broadbent gets is just like the tea of Shaw's childhood, drawn long on the hob, good and strong. Shaw himself, of course, never touched the stuff and, when discussing foreign trade in *The Intelligent Woman's Guide to Socialism and Capitalism*, he cannot resist an attack on the beverage that supports English and Irish life:

> *I will not add that we would have no tea, because I happen to think that we would be better without this insidious Chinese stimulant.*

John Bull's Other Island was originally written at the request of W B Yeats for The Abbey Theatre, but it proved too ambitious for his company, so it was performed in London where it was a smash hit. The term 'smash hit' is used advisedly, for King Edward VII laughed so much that he broke his chair in the Royal Box. The Irish engineer Larry Doyle is far cleverer than Broadbent, but he is cynical and disillusioned, believing that nothing can work successfully in a country of professional dreamers. But Broadbent, because he's a good sort of chap and means well and bumbles along happily (one of his attractions is that he is the sort of chap who needs hugs), is actually capable of realising his plans for Roscullen — plans that will turn the silent lake into a boating place, the fields into a golf course, and the desolate hillside into a luxury hotel. To Broadbent, Nora herself is a slender dream of desirable perfection. But Doyle cannot let him rest content with the romantic idea of her, and he lists what she eats:

> Breakfast: tea and bread-and-butter, with an occasional rasher, and an egg on special occasions: say on her birthday.
> Dinner in the middle of the day, one course and nothing else: in the evening, tea and bread-and-butter again. You compare her with your Englishwoman who wolfs down from three to five meat meals a day; and naturally you find her a sylph. The difference is not a difference of type: it's the difference between the woman who eats not wisely but too well and the woman who eats not wisely but too little.

There speaks Shaw the dietician on an adequate diet for women, who once wrote:

> A woman's mind is more wonderful than her flesh; but if her flesh is not fed, her mind will perish, whereas if you feed her flesh, her mind will take care of itself and of her flesh as well. Food comes first.

Food has more emotional connotations in *A Village Wooing*, a play structured in three conversations between **A** and **Z**, a man and a woman. When **A** comes into **Z**'s village shop and orders chocolate and cheese and apples, Hovis, butter and almonds accompanied by buttermilk and gingerbeer, **Z** decides he is to be her partner in marriage and in business. **A** eventually concedes a minor victory to the sensuous pleasures:

> Here in his shop I have everything that can gratify the senses: apples, onions and acid drops; pepper and mustard; long comforters and hot water bottles.

But in the end, the apotheosis he proposes for them both is beyond the physical when

> the world of the senses will vanish; and for us there will be nothing ridiculous, nothing uncomfortable, nothing unclean, nothing but pure paradise.

An entire luncheon is served on stage in *You Never Can Tell* by an omniscient waiter who rejoices in the name of Balmy Walters, and who, before the final curtain, gets the last word. The play deals with the paradoxes of social conventions. And what can be more conventional than a luncheon served in a hotel? The successive courses of soup, turbot, chicken, dessert and cheese appear in nicely judged counterpoint as Mrs Clandon attempts to sort out impossible family confusions. The wise waiter (Cyril Cusack played him to perfection in the Abbey show a few years ago) assists in the muddlesome discussion:

Dolly:	*Is your son a waiter too, William?*
Waiter:	*[serving Gloria with fowl] Oh no, Miss, he's too impetuous. He's at the Bar.*
McComas:	*[patronizingly] A potman, eh?*
Waiter:	*[with a touch of melancholy, as if really a disappointment softened by time] No, sir, the other bar. Your profession, sir. A Q.C., sir.*

On 1 June 1898, Bernard Shaw married Charlotte Payne-Townshend, 'the Irish lady with the pale green eyes and the million of money'. She had returned from Italy and found him in his squalid room in Fitzroy Square, extremely ill from a putrid infection in his foot that was attacking the bone. She took him over and nursed him, blaming part of his ill-health on his vegetarianism and part on his uncaring mother. To the surprise of all their friends, Shaw decided that the best way Charlotte could nurse him respectably would be to marry him. In typically Shavian fashion he wrote up the event himself for the *Star* newspaper:

As a lady and gentleman were out driving in Henrietta-st., Covent-garden yesterday, a heavy shower drove them to take shelter in the office of the Superintendent Registrar there, and in the confusion of the moment he married them. The lady was an Irish lady named Miss Payne-Townshend, and the gentleman was George Bernard Shaw.

Mr Graham Wallas and Mr H.S. Salt were also driven by stress of weather into the registrar's, and the latter being secretary of the Humanitarian League would naturally have remonstrated against the proceedings had there been time, but there wasn't. Mr Bernard Shaw means to go off to the country next week to recuperate, and this is the second operation he has undergone lately, not by a registrar, but by a surgeon.

Startling as was the liberty undertaken by the Henrietta-st. official, it turns out well. Miss Payne-Townshend is an Irish lady with an income many times the volume of that which 'Corno di Bassetto' used to earn, but to that happy man, being a vegetarian, the circumstance is of no moment. The lady is deeply interested in the London School of Economics, and that is the common ground on which the brilliant couple met. Years of married bliss to them.'

Although not a vegetarian herself, Mrs Shaw always made sure that Shaw's food was right for him. And Shaw, who had no time for living the life of the idle rich, who deprecated their silly activities and thought January strawberries tasted like corks, valued his cook:

I am like Molière in point of always consulting my cook about my plays. She is an excellent critic, goes to his lectures and plays, and esteems actors and actresses as filthy rags in comparison to the great author they interpret.

Mrs Shaw entertained a great deal and there was always meat and wine on the table. Shaw was served separately by a parlourmaid, he usually drank water or milk with the thirst of a healthy dog. At last he was cared for by an ideal companion; 'We are all women's babies,' he said, and Charlotte's only drawback was a passion for foreign travel, one of his worst dreads.

As he grew older, his appetite for sweet things increased; he loved cakes, whether of the fruity variety or covered with thick icing. Afternoon tea was always served in their home, with Shaw drinking milk and consuming innumerable chocolate biscuits. Desserts were sweetened with honey, for which he had a craving, perhaps a need dating from a childhood barren of treats. But, despite his sweet tooth, Shaw was extremely weight-conscious and counted the calories in all his meals, although whether he counted the calories that stuffed his pockets in the form of dried fruit and jelly babies, only he knows!

Shaw received a voluminous post-bag. One of the most common questions put to him concerned the nature of his vegetarian diet, to which he would reply with a standard postcard:

VEGETARIAN DIET

Mr Shaw's correspondents are reminded that current vegetarianism does not mean living wholly on vegetables. Vegetarians eat cheese, butter, honey, eggs and, on occasion, cod liver oil.

On this diet, without tasting fish, flesh or fowl, Mr Shaw has reached the age of 92 (1948) in as good condition as his meat eating contemporaries. It is beyond question that persons who have never from their birth been fed otherwise than as vegetarians are at no disadvantage, mentally, physically, nor in duration of life, with their carnivorous fellow-citizens.

Nevertheless Mr Shaw is of the opinion that his diet included an excess of protein. Until he was seventy he accumulated some poison that exploded every month or six weeks in a headache that blew it off and left him quite well after disabling him for a day. He tried every available treatment to get rid of the headaches, all quite unsuccessful. He now makes uncooked vegetables, chopped or grated, and their juices, with fruit, the staple of his diet, and finds it markedly better than the old high protein diet of beans, lentils and macaroni.

His objection to carnivorous diet is partly aesthetic, partly hygienic, mainly as involving an unnecessary waste of the labour of masses of mankind in the nurture and slaughter of cattle, poultry, and fish for human food.

He has no objection to the slaughter of animals as such. He knows that if we do not kill animals they will kill us. Squirrels, foxes, rabbits, tigers, cobras, locusts, white ants, rats, mosquitoes, fleas, and deer must be continually slain even to extermination by vegetarians as ruthlessly as by meat eaters. But he urges humane killing and does not enjoy it as a sport.

Ayot Saint Lawrence, Welwyn, Hertfordshire

He was adamant about remaining thin; there is a story that the corpulent Alfred Hitchcock said that, just by looking at Shaw, he knew there was still famine in Ireland. Shaw replied 'One look at you, Mr Hitchcock, and I know who caused it'.

George Bernard Shaw died at the age of 94 after a fall in the garden of his house, Shaw's Corner at Ayot St Lawrence, his longevity and health an advertisement for the diet that he had maintained for seventy years. His description of his own funeral has to be the most endearing of mortal visions:

My situation is a solemn one. Life is offered to me on condition of eating beefsteaks. My weeping family crowd about me with Bovril and Brand's Essence. But death is better than cannibalism. My will contains directions for my funeral, which will be followed not by mourning coaches, but by herds of oxen, sheep, swine, flocks of poultry, and a small travelling aquarium of live fish, all wearing white scarves in honour of the man who perished rather than eat his fellow-creatures. It will be, with the exception of the procession into Noah's Ark, the most remarkable thing of the kind ever seen.

PINHEAD OATMEAL PORRIDGE

Broadbent: By the way, you told me I couldn't have porridge for
breakfast; but Mr Doyle has some.
Hodson: Yes, sir. Very sorry, sir. They call it stirabout, sir,
that's how it was. They know no better, sir.
John Bull's Other Island

As you might have gathered by now, Shaw insists on having his opinion heard, on or off the soap-box, and is always prompt to provide appropriate advice, so we'll let him take over:

Boil oatmeal porridge for 20 minutes; and if you think the result mere oatmeal and water, try boiling it for two hours. If you still think it as unpalatable as dry bread, treat it as you treat the bread; stir up a bounteous lump of butter in it, and do not forget the salt. In eating wheatmeal porridge, remember that there's nothing so becomes a man as moderation and an admixture of stewed fruit.

> 1 cup pinhead oatmeal
> 3 cups cold water
> pinch of salt

Place the ingredients in a heavy pot. Bring to the boil and simmer for approximately 20 minutes, until thick. This makes a nutty, chewy porridge, lovely with salt or honey and cream. (The instructions on some packets of pinhead oatmeal produce something that looks like Dickensian gruel; ignore them.)

We prefer the other sort of porridge, stone-ground oatflakes, which make a smoother porridge, which also has a good flavour.

> 1 cup stoneground oatflakes
> 3 cups cold water
> pinch of salt

For this, use the same amount of water and a pinch of salt, but it cooks much faster, in about 10 minutes. Serve with demerara sugar and cream.
Serves two to four.

BROWN BREAD

Remember that brown bread is a good familiar creature, and worth more than its weight in flesh. Don't attribute every qualm you feel to a breakdown of your constitution for want of meat.

The only happy childhood memory Shaw had was of the one or two rare occasions his mother cut brown bread for him and buttered it 'thickly instead of merely wiping a knife on it'.

There seem to be as many brown bread recipes in Ireland as there are breadmakers, and everyone swears by their own. This one belongs to Veronica's Aunty Mary, who makes the best brown soda bread ever. At her home it is eaten with her own loganberry jam, made from home-grown loganberries — very heaven!

12oz (360g) wholemeal flour
4oz (120g) white flour
1 tbsp wheatgerm
1 level tsp bicarbonate of soda
pinch of salt
1 egg, beaten
1/2 pt (300ml) buttermilk

Preheat oven to 200°C (400°F, Gas mark 6).

Combine the flour, wheatgerm, bicarbonate of soda and salt in a large mixing bowl. Add the egg and buttermilk and mix well with a knife. Turn out on a board, knead and shape into a round about 3 inches thick. Cut a cross on the top. Place on a greased baking tin and dust the top of the bread with flour. Bake for 40 minutes at 200°C (400°F, Gas mark 6), or until the base sounds hollow when tapped. Makes one loaf.

VEGETABLE CASSEROLE

Vegetarian diet helps people to keep their tempers instead of wasting them on useless anger and sputtering. It saves and conserves temper; and temper is life. Most people haven't half temper enough, and the little they have they waste because they keep it on a diet of stout and oysters, or steak and porter.

This vegetable casserole may or may not keep your temper in prime condition, but it is easy to make and good to eat with baked potatoes. If a hot temper is your desire, then add lots of spices for a more piquant flavour. As Shaw advises:

If you want fancy dishes, make them for yourself out of plainly cooked vegetables, with the help of rice and the cruet stand; and do not be seduced by messy pies, entrées or such weak concessions to the enemy as 'vegetable rabbit', 'vegetable sausage' or the like.

3 onions	½lb (240g) mushrooms
2½ tbsp oil	1 400g tin tomatoes
2 large leeks	1 tin flageolet beans
3 sticks celery	salt and pepper
2 small red peppers	chopped parsley
3 carrots	

Preheat oven to 180°C (350°F, Gas mark 4).

Prepare and chop all the vegetables. In a heavy casserole, fry the onions gently in the oil, followed by the leeks and celery. Then add the red peppers, carrots and mushrooms.* Sweat these with the lid on for 20 minutes, then add the tomatoes and beans and season well. Cover the casserole and bake for 40 to 50 minutes. Sprinkle with a good handful of chopped parsley and serve with rice.

*For a spicy vegetable casserole, add 1 tablespoon of curry powder at this point or, if you prefer, the following curry spices:

2 crushed cardamom pods	1 clove garlic, finely chopped
1 tsp turmeric	¼ tsp crushed chilli
½ tsp crushed cumin seeds	
1 tsp fresh chopped ginger *or* ½ tsp ginger powder	

Serves six.

MACARONI

Mangan:	What a dinner! I don't call it a dinner, I call it a meal.
Ellie:	I am accustomed to meals, Mr Mangan, and very lucky to get them. Besides the captain cooked some macaroni for me.
Mangan:	[shuddering liverishly] Too rich: I can't eat such things.

Heartbreak House

Fionn's sister Orla is the only person we have ever met who, when living in the country, used to cook all the meals over an open fire. Sponges and even Christmas cakes worked like a dream. She always said it was a great excuse for sitting by the fire during the chilly Wicklow winters. This is her macaroni recipe.

8oz (240g) macaroni
1 tsp salt
4 pt (2l) water
4 bacon rashers
2 tbsp sunflower oil
3 eggs
4 tbsp cream
pinch of nutmeg
$1/4$ tsp cayenne pepper
salt and pepper
4oz (120g) grated cheddar cheese
handful of chopped parsley

Cook the macaroni by boiling in 2 litres of salted water for 15 minutes. Drain it in a colander and rinse well under hot running water. Chop the bacon rashers and fry in oil for 3 minutes. Beat the eggs with the cream, nutmeg and cayenne pepper and season with salt and pepper. Add to the rashers and scramble lightly, stirring briskly. Add the grated cheese and sprinkle with chopped parsley. Put the macaroni in a serving dish and pour the sauce over it.
Serves four.

VEGETABLE GOOSE WITH IBSEN SAUCE

Grace: A woman belongs to herself and to nobody else.
Charteris: Quite right. Ibsen for ever! That's exactly my
              opinion. Now, tell me, do I belong to Julia; or have I
              a right to belong to myself?
Grace: [puzzled] Of course you have, but —
Charteris: [interrupting her triumphantly] Then how can you
              steal me from Julia if I don't belong to her?
              [He catches her by the shoulders and holds her out
              at arm's length in front of him] Eh, little
              philosopher? No, my dear: if Ibsen sauce is good for
              the goose, it's good for the gander as well.'

The Philanderer

In this case the goose is the worthy marrow. Shaw calls it 'vegetable goose' and recommends that it should be filled with sage stuffing. Shaw was the first dramatist to introduce Ibsenite ideas to the English theatre. *The Philanderer* satirises the pseudo-Ibsenites at a London Club where the 'advanced women' perplex the pathetic dinosaurs of men. Ibsen sauce? Simply stewed apple — it's always worth getting to the core of Shavian philosophy.

     1 medium-sized vegetable marrow

Preheat oven to 150°C (300°F, Gas Mark 2).

Cut in half lengthways, scoop out the seeds, stuff each side, then bake side by side in a greased baking tin.

Stuffing

     2oz (60g) butter
     2 large onions, chopped
     4oz (120g) walnuts, crushed
     4oz (120g) breadcrumbs
     1 tsp each chopped sage and thyme
     handful of chopped parsley
     salt and pepper

Melt the butter in a saucepan, then add the onions. Cover, and cook gently to soften the onions. Add the walnuts and fry until brown. Remove from the heat, add the rest of the ingredients, season and mix well together. Stuff the marrow and bake at 150°C (300°F, Gas mark 2) for 2 hours.

Apple Sauce

     1lb (480g) cooking apples, peeled, cored and sliced
     2 tbsp water
     ½oz (15g) butter
     juice of ½ lemon
     1oz (30g) sugar

Stew the apples very gently with the water and butter until soft. Beat them until smooth. Add the lemon juice and sugar.
Serves four.

POSH RICE PUDDING

Waiter: Cheese, sir? Or would you like a cold sweet?
Crampton: [taken aback] What? Oh! Cheese, cheese.

You Never Can Tell

Cold sweet does not sound overly tempting but this one is an empress among puds — a classic French dish called *Riz à l'Imperatrice*. It is traditionally made with candied fruit but we think fresh fruit is far nicer. Posh rice pudding is good enough for the classiest of dinner parties, and Shaw, who liked rice and had an incredibly sweet tooth, would probably have adored it.

8oz (240g) short grain rice
3 pt (1½l) milk
2 eggs, separated
8oz (240g) castor sugar
1 packet 5g powdered gelatine
2 chopped apples
2 chopped oranges
2 sliced bananas
¼lb (120g) grapes, halved and pipped
½pt (300ml) cream, whipped
1lb (480g) raspberries
sugar to taste

Cook the rice with 2 pints (1l) of milk very gently until all the milk is absorbed. Do not cover the pot. Then add the remaining milk and stir into the rice until it is creamy and mushy. Beat the egg yolks and sugar until pale. Dissolve the gelatine in 2 tbsp of very hot but not boiling water, then add to the beaten egg yolks. Put the cooked rice in a large mixing bowl and allow to cool. Then stir in the egg yolk mixture. Beat the egg whites and fold into the rice; add the chopped fruit and, lastly, the whipped cream. Transfer to a large serving dish and refrigerate until set. Serve with raspberry purée.

Liquidise the raspberries, then rub through a sieve to remove the pips. Sweeten to taste and serve chilled.
Serves six.

3

Somerville and Ross

Edith Somerville and **Martin Ross** were second cousins who met in their twenties in St Barrahane's Church in Castletownshend, County Cork, an enclave of the ascendancy class and Somerville's home. Edith Somerville was a Paris-trained artist and illustrator and Violet Martin (known as Martin) was a journalist, but an urgent need to supplement their incomes inspired them to write a cheap 'shocker', *An Irish Cousin* (1889). This was followed by novels, travel books and short stories. *The Real Charlotte* (1894) is arguably the best Irish novel of the period, and the ever-popular *Some Experiences of an Irish RM* established them as best-seller authors and ensured their immortality as writers. Ross died in 1915 but Edith believed that she communicated from beyond the grave, thus the remarkable literary collaboration continued until Edith's death at the age of ninety-one.

Somerville and Ross

1858 to 1949
1862 to 1915

> We drew forth the half-bottle of Grand St Lambert that had for
> the last few days been carried perilously about in a bonnet-box,
> and with grapes and croissants began a repast that continued
> through stages of Bovril, tea and ginger bread biscuits until we
> neared Paris.
>
> *In the Vine Country*

Somerville and Ross were no gourmets; they were, however, tea-drinking
addicts with a rather absent-minded attitude to food. The cousins made
many expeditions together ('...times of the best when we went where we
would and did what pleased us most') and wrote them up as magazine
articles, which eventually were published as guide books. Delicious meals
are never described in detail on the French or Danish tours; nasty ones are,
as when they sampled *cèpes* 'which resembled sweetbreads and cut rather
like tough custard pudding. It was fried light brown, but the inside was
yellowish white and the whole thing was swimming in oil...a dreadful taste,
as though rotten leaves and a rusty knife had been fried together in fat.'

In the Vine Country recounts their adventures in France — the
discomforts of foreign travel were only marginally relieved by frequent cups
of tea (they brought their own spirit lamp, kettle and English tea). The
French hoteliers attempted to sabotage this necessary pleasure by boiling
the milk, thus incensing Somerville. Even breakfast, that most harmless of
French meals, is accompanied by battalions of flies. A constant fear is the
horror of consuming *compôtes* of grease and garlic, and doubts in
restaurants are solved by always ordering *oeufs sur le plat*. The culinary
highspot of the vineyards tour is an *omelette au rhum*, pronounced delicious
by both. Somerville and Ross, fearless doyennes of the hunting field, were
cowardly eaters.

Somerville and Ross were second cousins and belonged to the
comfortable world of the Protestant ascendancy. They did not meet until
'well-stricken in years': Violet Martin (pen-name Ross, always referred to as
Martin by Edith) was just twenty and Edith four years older, 'not absolutely
the earliest morning of life; say about half-past 10 o'clock, with breakfast
(and all traces of bread and butter) cleared away'.

Edith was already established as a painter and illustrator; Martin was a
journalist. Their combined talents, coupled with profound affection,

created a literary collaboration celebrated all over the world, particularly as the creators of the famous RM stories.

They shared the supreme passion of hunting. Edith was the first woman MFH (Master of Fox Hounds) in Ireland ('No money for stockings but keep hounds. How very Irish.') and the ecstasy and adventure inspire many of their stories, distilling the very wine of life. Little dogs too are a pleasure; they considered writing a dog-novel, tempted by the notion of entitling it *Kennelworth!* It is after hunting, soaked through and frozen to the bone-marrow, that the Somerville and Ross company of endearing and enduring characters, Major Yeates and Flurry and all the others, drink their scalding tea and hot whiskey and eat anything that is going in order to combat the miseries of Irish winter weather and an outdoor life. In the Royal Hotel, waiting and starving for a meal ordered two hours before, 'the air was charged with the mingled odours of boiling cabbage and frying mutton; we affected to speak of them with disgust, but our souls yearned for them'. So too did Edith and Martin; food was for re-fuelling during the business of a very active life. When Edith was a student at Calarossi's studio in Paris, she described with relish the delicious French-fried potatoes she would buy for five sous and carry home wrapped in a copy of *La Patrie*.

Both women ran Big Houses. Edith was mistress of Drishane, in Castletownshend, West Cork, and Martin was in charge, for a long period, of Ross House in County Galway. Their housekeeping experiences, peculiar to Irish Big House living, provided a brilliant blueprint for 'Shreelane', Major Yeates' house in *Some Experiences of an Irish RM*. Drishane had an endemic rat problem, and at Shreelane the holes are nailed up with pieces of tin biscuit boxes, and there is 'ceaseless warfare with drains, eaveshoots, chimneys, pumps', and a visitor could easily write his name in the damp of the walls.

Edith and Martin shared an endearing weakness; they were both martyrs to the *fou rire*, that uncontrollable fit of giggles that leaves the victim incapable and helpless. Edith said 'Martin and I were not accustomed to taking ourselves seriously', and they give Philippa Yeates the dubious gift of 'unsuitable laughter':

She regarded Shreelane and its floundering, foundering ménage of incapables in the light of a gigantic picnic in a foreign land.

Philippa's relations with her cook, the unsurpassable Mrs Cadogan, are fraught with incapacitating attacks of the giggles, as Mrs Cadogan makes unreasonable demands of the English language and of her own surprising cuisine:

'Bridgie! Where's me beautiful head and me lovely feet?'
'Bilin' in the pot, ma'am.'

Philippa was having a dinner party, and the animal extremities were merely soup 'in its elemental stage'. But the menu becomes problematic when the fish are delivered. The fish in question are 'leppin' fresh' and the RM asks Mrs Cadogan whether she wants them.

'What fish is it, Sir?' replied Mrs Cadogan presenting at the kitchen window a face like a harvest moon.
'Tis pollock, ma'am!' shouted Mrs Brickley from the foot of the steps.
"Sha! thim's no good to us!' responded the harvest moon in bitter scorn.
'Thim's not company fish.'

The RM compares eating pollock to eating boiled cotton wool with pins in it, but Philippa prevails and pollock is served filleted in white sauce.

It is not that Somerville and Ross were uninterested in food — their work abounds in descriptions of breakfasts, luncheons, teas and dinners — but the meals are there because they provide such marvellous comic opportunities, rich situations for the sort of humorous writing in which they excelled. Revolting meals are described with glee and disgusted relish:

A meal that had opened at six with strong tea, cold mutton and bottled porter, was still, at eight o'clock, in slow but increasing progress, suggesting successive inspirations on the part of the cook. At about seven we had had mutton chops and potatoes and now, after an abysmal interval of conversation, we were faced by a roast goose and a rice pudding with currants in it.

Or Miss Shute at a country inn:

She delicately moved the potato dish so as to cover the traces of a bygone egg, and her glance lingered on the flies that dragged their way across a melting mound of salt butter. 'I like local colour, but I don't care for it on the table cloth.'

Or when the naughty water spaniel, Maria, steals the roast beef:

'And I had planned that bit of beef for the lunches,' continued Mrs Cadogan in impassioned lamentation, 'the way we wouldn't have to inthrude on the

cold turkey! Sure he has it that dhragged, that all we can do with it now is
run it through the mincing machine for the Major's sandwiches.'

Somerville and Ross were the chroniclers of an Ireland now vanished. The
country social life of Victorian Ireland is all there to enjoy and to amaze the
reader. You can discover what was eaten at hunt balls, servants' dances, and
dinner at the Big House. After the ball in *An Irish Cousin,* a bottle of
champagne is put into each departing coach to alleviate the rigours of the
journey home. In *The Real Charlotte* 'tea at Mrs Beattie's parties was a
serious meal', the wonderful yearly harvest of raspberries being an ideal
chance to attract potential suitors for the daughters. And of course, there
were innumerable picnics.

Philippa nurtures 'an inappeasable passion for picnics'; undaunted by the
rigours, she is able to 'tackle a moist chicken pie with a splinter of slate and
my stylograph pen'. For Francie in *The Real Charlotte*, it is her ideal milieu,
an opportunity for flirting and fun:

> *Francie was sitting on a mossy bank, a little away from the table-cloth, with*
> *a plate of cherry pie on her lap, Mr Hawkins at her feet, and unlimited*
> *opportunities for practical jestings with the cherry-stones.*

Somerville and Ross, inveterate, experienced travellers as they were, relished
the exigencies of the picnic experience.

> *There is something unavoidably vulgar in the aspect of a picnic party when*
> *engaged in the culminating rite of eating on the grass. They may feel*
> *themselves to be picturesque, gypsy-like, even romantic, but to the*
> *unparticipating looker-on, not even the gilded dignity of champagne can*
> *redeem them from being a mere group of greedy huddled backs, with ugly*
> *trimmings of papers, dirty plates and empty bottles.*

In *Some Irish Yesterdays,* an entire chapter is devoted to picnics, with special
attention given to the horrors of yachting picnics, when luncheon baskets
are always either mislaid or ship-bound on becalmed boats and everyone
either starves to death or ends up in a ghastly pub drinking sour porter and
eating stale biscuits.

Edith's first memory of a picnic was an illicit one in the company of two
turf-boys; they ate 'something disgusting with carraway seeds in it, kneaded
by our own filthy hands' (and drank) 'stolen claret from the dining room'.

But despite the vicissitudes, Somerville ends her essay on picnics on a lyrical note,

> *I maintain that the ideal picnic is only achieved by the most super-civilised elimination and selection. Two, or at most four, congenial souls, and a tea basket of latest device and most expert equipment — these things, and thoroughly dry grass and I ask no more of heaven.*

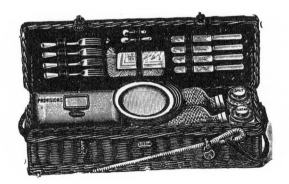

POTTED MEATS

A great many people have asked us why we did not make our
journey through Connemara on bicycles: the roads are so good,
the mail cars offer such facilities for the transport of baggage, the
speed and simplicity are so great. To this we have our reply —
what then of the luncheon hamper? These objections have not
taken into account the comfortable wayside halt by the
picturesque and convenient lake; the unpacking of the spirit lamp
and its glittering bride, the tin kettle, the dinner knives at six
pence apiece, the spoons at twopence halfpenny, the potted
meats, the Bath Olivers, the Bovril and the Burgundy.

Through Connemara in a Governess Cart

Recently, in his column 'Dubliner's Diary' in the *Irish Times*, Kevin Myers
bemoaned the demise of home-made potted meats in the Irish diet. They are
delicious and easy to make, and this recipe is for him.

Before food processors were invented, making potted meat was a labour-
intensive activity: the meat had to be cooked, chopped fine and then pounded to a
paste. No light undertaking, when preparing for a picnic. Thanks to modern
technology, a food processor will do the job in an instant.

The following recipe offers a sandwich filling that is both nutritious and
popular and, if presented in ramekins and served with brown bread and lemon
wedges, makes a very attractive starter.

> 4oz (120g) cooked chicken
> nutmeg
> 2oz (60g) cooked ham or bacon
> mace
> 1½oz (45g) butter
> salt and pepper

Process the meats separately. Season the chicken with nutmeg and the ham with
mace. Place the meat, 1oz (25g) of butter per 4oz (120g) of meat, the seasoning and
salt and pepper in the food processor, and process with a sharp blade. It will very
quickly reduce to a breadcrumb texture. Place the mixture in a bowl and press
firmly with a wooden spoon to form a paste.

If you wish to keep potted meat, place in ramekins; a layer of the chicken
mixture, a layer of ham, and another of chicken to finish. Leave some room to cover
the top of the paste with about a quarter of an inch of melted butter. Allow to set
and store in the fridge.

Makes ¾ cup.

POTATO CAKES

While I live I shall not forget her potato cakes. They came in hot
and hot from a pot-oven, they were speckled with caraway seeds,
they swam in salt butter, and we ate them shamelessly and
greasily, and washed them down with hot whisky and water. I
knew to a nicety how ill I should be next day, and I heeded not.
Some Experiences of an Irish RM

Potato cakes are one of the staple foods in Irish literature. We've found them in the
works of Joyce, Kate O'Brien, George Birmingham and even Shaw. They are really
comforting and filling on a cold winter's day, and everyone in our families loves
them.

    4 freshly cooked potatoes
    salt and pepper
    1oz (30g) butter
    chopped onion and parsley make an interesting flavour
    2oz (60g) flour

Potato cakes must be made with floury potatoes. In Ireland, a consistently floury
variety is the Record, but Kerr's Pinks come as an unreliable second choice.

Mash the potatoes with the seasoning and the butter, and add half a chopped
onion and a tablespoon of parsley if desired. Add the flour and mix well.

Turn onto a floured board and knead until smooth. Divide in two. Roll out into
a circle of about ¼in thickness and cut it into triangles. Fry on a preheated, heavy,
well-greased pan until browned on both sides.
Serves four.

BAKED SALMON

Detestable soup in a splendid old silver tureen that was nearly as dark in hue as Robinson Crusoe's thumb; a perfect salmon, perfectly cooked, on a chipped kitchen dish; such cut glass as is not easy to find nowadays; stew that, as Flurry subsequently remarked, would burn the shell off an egg; and a bottle of port, draped in immemorial cobwebs, wan with age, and probably priceless.

Some Experiences of an Irish RM

One cannot conceive of Irish cuisine without the king of fish, the salmon of knowledge. Irish salmon is arguably the best in the world. There cannot be a nicer lunch than thinly sliced smoked salmon with freshly made brown bread, accompanied by a glass or two of Guinness's stout.

> 1 salmon
> 2oz (60g) butter
> salt and pepper
> sprig each of parsley, thyme, oregano, marjoram, fennel

Preheat oven to 175°C (350°F, Gas mark 4).

Gut the salmon but leave the head on. Clean out the blood carefully and rinse the fish under a cold tap. Lay it on two layers of tin foil that are at least twice the length of the fish. Butter the inside of the fish and season with pepper and salt. Stuff it with the herbs. Fresh herbs are preferable, dried ones just do not work. Wrap the fish well in the tinfoil, folding it over to ensure it is as water tight a parcel as possible.

Place the fish in as large a baking tin as will fit in your oven. If the fish is too big, curl it around on its side to fit.

Bake for 15 minutes per pound.

Remove from the tin and straighten the parcel out before it cools. When cool, unwrap the fish and skin it. If, however, the salmon is for a party or a buffet, you might wish to decorate it. First remove the head. Cut the fish along the back bone and lift off the top half carefully. Then remove the spine and bones from the lower half. Check for loose bones. Reassemble the two halves with the head on a serving dish. The traditional way of decorating a salmon is to cover it with mayonnaise and place thinly sliced cucumber on top, arranged as fish scales.

Allow 6oz per person.

LEFTOVER PIE

'Mary!' She said with awful brevity, 'Major Anderson has come
back!' 'Lord God Almighty!' responded the Monkey, very
appositely flinging both her arms over her head... 'Clear the
kitchen!' She said with a majestic sweep of one fat arm... There
was soup, but there was nothing hot. 'There must be an entrée,'
says Sylvia. 'I have nothing in the place, Ma'am,' says the Monkey.
'The chicken pie!' said the inspired Sylvia. Its insides were clawed
out of it and hurled into a bowl of curry, the lobster salad was
similarly disembowelled, devilled and sent in as a savoury.
                The Selected Letters of Somerville and Ross, ed. Gifford Lewis

Edith made short shrift of both leftovers and boring vicars. On one occasion she
was seated at the organ at St Barrahane's Church (where she was organist for
seventy years) listening to a seemingly endless sermon on the decadence of the
Ottoman Empire. Reaching a rhetorical peak the vicar cried, 'What shall we do
with this decayed Turkey?' From the organ loft a penetrating voice suggested,
'Curry it, you fool, curry it.'

The curry appeared with monotonous frequency on the table of the Big House
— a sort of hangover from the British Raj and the ideal method of dealing with
rabbits and leftovers; Martin, we are told, sent them 'to heaven in a curry as in a
chariot of fire'. Old Mrs Knox of Aussolas served curries that would take the splint
off a horse.

We are no Madhur Jaffreys so we're going to do the opposite of the Monkey in
the emergency, and put the leftovers into the pie with not a pinch of curry powder
in sight. Perverse, but you see neither of us eat curried dishes.

> 1lb (480g) cooked chicken
> ½lb (240g) cooked ham or bacon
> 2 leeks, chopped
> ½lb (240g) sausage meat
> 2 hardboiled eggs
> leftover vegetables (e.g. potatoes, onions, peas, carrots)
> 1 pt (600ml) stock or gravy
> savory and thyme
> salt and pepper
> 1 pkt puff pastry
> 1 egg, beaten

Preheat oven to 200°C (400°F, Gas mark 6).

Grease a large pie-dish. Chop the chicken and ham. Add the chopped leek to the sausage meat. Slice the hard-boiled eggs. Put the chicken meat in a layer on the bottom of the pie dish, followed by the ham and then the sausage meat mixture. Next put in a layer of sliced hard-boiled egg, followed by the leftover vegetables (avoid the brassica family); pour in the stock, add the herbs and season. Cover with a lid of pastry, making a hole in the top for steam to escape, and brush with beaten egg.

Bake for 30 to 40 minutes until the pastry is golden brown.

Serves six.

VICTORIAN SPONGE CAKE

> Norry was not to be seen, but on the table were bowls with flour, eggs and sugar and beside them was laid a bunch of twigs, tied together like a miniature birch rod. The making of a sponge cake was one of Francie's few accomplishments, and putting on an apron of dubious cleanliness, lent by Louisa, she began operations by breaking the eggs, separating the yolks from the whites, and throwing the shells into the fire with professional accuracy of aim.
>
> *The Real Charlotte*

Fionn's father, besides being a sculptor and painter, was a consummate maker of sponges; high and light and squashy. The following recipe should give you that result, and will certainly not taste like the Somerville and Ross description of a shop cake, 'the usual conglomerate of tallow, sawdust, bad eggs and gravel'.

9oz (270g) sugar
juice and grated rind of half a lemon
7oz (210g) flour
5 eggs, separated

Preheat oven to 180°C (350°F, Gas mark 4).

Beat egg whites first and set aside. Beat egg yolks very well until pale yellow. Then add the sugar, lemon juice and rind to the egg yolks. Keep beating until the egg yolks have greatly increased in volume and are thick and pale.

Fold in the egg whites very gently. Sieve the flour onto the mixture and fold in gently. Pour into two greased and floured 9in (22cm) tins.

Bake for 30 minutes.

Remove from oven and leave for a few minutes to set. Then turn onto a wire rack to cool. Split the cakes in two and fill with jam and cream.

Makes two layers.

TIPSY TRIFLE

> Of its component parts I can only remember that there was a
> soup tureen full of custard, a mountainous dish of trifle, in whose
> veins ran honey, instead of jam, and to whose enlivenment a
> bottle at least of whiskey had been dedicated.
>
> *Further Experiences of an Irish RM*

This trifle, though not the one at Mrs McRory's agonising dinner, is of the very large variety, and we found that a big soup tureen was the best dish for it. The recipe is a Victorian one, very boozy, and the result rather popular. Fionn's mother Frances said there was never a trifle like it. That is the truth!

1lb (480g) sponge cake, one day old
$^{1}/_{2}$lb (240g) jam of your choice
$^{1}/_{2}$ pt (300ml) sweetish sherry
$^{1}/_{2}$ wine glass brandy
$^{1}/_{2}$ wine glass liqueur of choice
3oz (90g) sugar
1 pt (600ml) milk
6 eggs
1 pear*
1 banana*
1 apple*
1 orange*
$^{1}/_{2}$tsp vanilla essence
1 pt (600ml) whipped cream
1oz (30g) toasted almonds

* or fruit in season

Two 9in (22cm) sponge tins make about 1lb (480g) sponge, though good shop ones would do. Spread jam to cover sponge and cut into square chunks. Take a large serving dish and place one layer of the sponge on the bottom. Combine the sherry and spirits and pour about $^{1}/_{6}$ of it over the sponge, then make another layer, until the sponge and booze are all gone.

Make a custard as follows: dissolve 3oz of sugar in the milk. Beat the eggs and add to the milk in a dribble while the milk heats but does not boil — stirring rapidly all the time. Return saucepan to low heat for about 10 minutes, until it begins to thicken, stirring constantly. Take it off the heat the second it begins to thicken or it will curdle (have an ice cube handy in case it does). Chop the fruit and place on top of the sponge. Add the vanilla to the custard and stir. Allow to cool completely, then spoon the custard on top of the fruit. Lastly whip the cream, spread it on top of the custard and decorate with toasted almonds. Fionn decorates trifle with heartsease or comfrey flowers.

Serves eight.

4

Oliver St John Gogarty

Oliver St John Gogarty, surgeon/poet and raconteur extraordinaire, was born in Dublin. He was a student friend of James Joyce, and was fossilised as Buck Mulligan in Joyce's novel *Ulysses*. Gogarty wrote the first 'slum play', entitled *Blight*, for the Abbey Theatre. His poetry is rich in classical allusion, ignoring modern trends and celebrating life and beauty. He crammed into one life many roles: doctor, writer, senator, aviator, hotelier, sportsman, lecturer, sensation seeker. He was a friend of W B Yeats, who considered him the greatest lyric poet of the age. His conversational inventiveness was legendary, belonging to that literary set that masterminded the Irish cultural renaissance. *As I Was Going Down Sackville Street* chronicles that period. He died in New York.

Oliver St John Gogarty 1878 to 1957

Why I hate food. It interrupts good talk, and just as I thought I
was making a good impression or just as I thought I was doing
well with my reactions...the waiter hisses, 'Sauce tartare?' Is it any
wonder I prefer drink to food.
As I Was Going Down Sackville Street

Conversation was Dr Gogarty's natural element; he revelled in it and was
unstoppable. Augustus John once threw a dish of peanuts at him in an
urgent effort to dam the flood of words. Food interfered with talk — it was
not that he disliked it, it was simply undeserving of his attention. A notable
wit and raconteur, he became a favourite of London Society hostesses in the
twenties when forced by perilous circumstances (attempted assassination
and the destruction by political fire of his Connemara home) to set up
practice there.

After Gogarty had lunched with Lady Ebury, an impressed and envious
George Moore asked him:

'What did you eat?'
'To tell you the truth, I never noticed. I talk too much.'
He threw up his hands. 'You are a barbarian. Tell her to ask me.'

But she didn't.

Yeats said Gogarty 'came drunk from his mother's womb'; life itself
seemed enough to inebriate him, and he remained on the dry from 1917
until he began writing professionally in the thirties. But he recalls happily
'the pleasant business of the glasses — the gay gurgling', and he is
associated forever with such hostelries as the Bailey which was the haunt of
Arthur Griffith, William Orpen, Seamus O'Sullivan and a host of wits and
poets, the Dolphin Restaurant, and of course Jammet's, the celebrated
restaurant where everyone who was anyone entertained their guests and
where Professor Yelverton Tyrrell followed his favourite lobster with
whiskey chasers.

Between 1915 and 1917 Oliver Gogarty had his rooms next door to the
Shelbourne Hotel, and years later a bar was opened there — some might

say appropriately. The Shelbourne bar was also the inspiration for 'The One Before Breakfast':

The one before breakfast
Alone in the Bar,
Will slide down your neck fast
And ease the catarrh
Your glass with its end up
Will scarce leave your jaws
When your body will send up
A round of applause.

On Friday nights the Gogartys were 'at home' to Dublin society. Mrs Neenie Gogarty presided over the tea urn and the methylated spirit burner in the corner of the drawingroom, AE sat on the sofa on the far side of the fire, and W B Yeats sat opposite, both engaged in competing for conversation space. Whiskey was available in the diningroom decanter for the drinkers.

When Oliver Gogarty became a senator in December 1922, Wednesday night became the 'dining in' night for senators at Ely Place. The kitchen was in the capable charge of Mrs Keely. Oliver Duane Gogarty, the eldest child, remembers the food as delicious, for Mrs Keely was a wonderful cook — her only drawback was her annual binge. An exasperated Mrs Gogarty once sent her to the boss for a ticking off. Mrs Keely explained that her friend had been visiting her, had taken a 'strong weakness' and could only be revived with a dozen Guinness — each! When she eventually retired years later she left the house with three cats in her suitcase.

Neenie Gogarty came from Connemara, and Oliver shared her love for the 'many coloured land'. He bought haunted Renvyle House in 1915 and a 'trembling Model T Ford' for the long drive. Augustus John painted there and Professor John Pentland Mahaffy described the sea as 'plum blue'. W B Yeats brought his bride to Renvyle House on their honeymoon; in a letter to Gogarty he said how much they were looking forward to their host's conversation, scenery and trout. The restless Gogarty found unexpected peace. After the house met the same fate as many great and beautiful Irish houses in the violent, bloody twenties, it was rebuilt and opened as a hotel. In 1930 Neenie was in charge; the visitor's book reveals an extraordinary collection of guests: aristocracy in large numbers, barons, countesses, earls and a French Marquis mixed with theatre people, W B Yeats, Augustus John, Count and Countess McCormack, and Alfred Byrne, Lord Mayor of

Dublin. Oliver Duane Gogarty (now a senior counsel and a Bencher of the Honorable Society of King's Inns) still remembers her speciality, lobster in a creamy sherry sauce.

The Gogartys owned a house on the island of Freilaun in Tully lake; a secret, magic place, hidden amidst lush vegetation. Oliver Duane Gogarty remembers living there for three months on rashers and bread from Tully village, and a lake full of brown trout.

Reading *As I Was Going Down Sackville Street* is the nearest thing to actually accompanying the master talker on one of his saunters around Dublin. He was a man of enthusiasm and irrepressible energy who knew simply everyone, and his son remembers how the short walk from Ely Place to the Shelbourne would take ages as he stopped and talked. The book reflects a life crowded with activity, incident and personality, and a man brimming over in his celebration of life. At the end of Sackville Street, as Gogarty dozes in the sunshine, the memory of himself as a little child comes to him:

> *with velvet suit and lace collar in a public-house tempted by a coachman and wondering at the drink proffered to him in secrecy, sweet and bitter, sanguine as Life.*
>
> *'Would you care for another raspberry cordial, Master Oliver?*
>
> *By' Gis and by St Charity, if it lead to a great calm like this above the world, with friends like these, in spite of the danger of its becoming a habit, I would say 'The Same Again' and chance again my lucky stars.*

TURBOT WITH LOBSTER SAUCE

Wallpaper like this, Jammet, with lobster sauce, unthinkable.
So Jammet got in a couple of bill-posters who valiantly posted up
some new wallpaper during the fish course.
A carpet of a different colour was provided with the game.
As I Was Going Down Sackville Street

Professor Tyrrell, the Benign Doctor who declared 'There is no such thing as a large whiskey' once gave a dinner at Jammet's Restaurant for five people at £8 a head. Before the First World War that was a princely sum for dining out. But the good Doctor found fault not with the turbot chosen for the fish course, but with the colour of the sauce which fought with the colour of the restaurant walls.

> 3lb (1½kg) turbot
> 1oz (30g) butter
> 2 shallots finely chopped
> juice of 1 lemon
> 1 wine glass dry white wine
> salt and pepper

Wash and trim the fish. Butter a baking dish and place the fish in with the rest of the ingredients. Cover with tin foil and bake for 25 to 30 minutes at 200°C (400°F, Gas mark 6). Remove the skin before serving.

Lobster Sauce

> 1½oz (45g) flour
> 1oz (30g) butter
> ½pt (300ml) stock using juices from the turbot, made up to ½ pt by
>   adding more wine
> ½pt (300 ml) cream
> salt and pepper
> 2oz (60g) lobster spawn
> ½ cooked lobster
> watercress, to garnish

Make a roux with the flour and butter. Add the stock, stirring all the time. Add the cream, salt and pepper, lobster spawn and lobster meat cut into small pieces. Stir constantly until the sauce thickens. Purée, pour over the turbot, and garnish with lots of watercress. This is the most expensive dish to make in our book.
Serves six.

SKATE ON FRIDAY

It was the long table (at the end of a long passage) full of boiling coffee, hot tripe and onions, skate (on Fridays) and crubeens that attracted the weary nightfarer.

Tumbling in the Hay

Life as a medical student in turn-of-the-century Dublin is the subject of *Tumbling in the Hay*. The Hay Hotel (so called because the window boxes were stuffed with hay for the cabbies' horses) was run by Stephen and Maria, once in the employ of Gogarty's father and dismissed when discovered *in flagrante delicto*. They provided refreshment for night owls; a welcoming haven for students and other vagrants enjoying a night's escapades in the Kips, Dublin's notorious red light district. Maria and Stephen dish up the hospitality amid scenes of comic chaos and Rabelaisian delight. The atmosphere belongs to the Middle Ages.

Bouillon

> 1 chopped onion
> 2½ pt (1¼l) water
> 1 chopped carrot
> a sprig each of parsley and thyme
> salt and pepper
>
> 4 skate wings
> 2oz (60g) butter
> salt and pepper

Make the bouillon by putting all the ingredients in a large saucepan and bringing it to the boil. Simmer for 30 minutes. Put the skate wings into the saucepan and poach for 10 to 15 minutes. Lift the skate out and place on a warmed dish. Melt the butter, add the salt and pepper, and pour over the fish.
Serves four.

COLLARED HEAD

I stole a glance at Mercédès and ordered a helping of collared head.

Tumbling in the Hay

Every Christmas John O'Mara of Irish Arctic Expedition fame creates an extraordinary beast called collared head. His recipe is a special one, handed down through the O'Maras, a Limerick family noted for their involvement in pigs and politics. Mrs Beeton offers a simple version, but John's, as Henry James would say, is the 'real thing', and as far as we know does not exist in any other cookery book. Known in the family as Clotted Death, it takes a weekend to make, so its rarity is unsurprising. On your own head be it!

The original recipe is from Limerick. Collared Head is a spiced brawn which looks like a salami-type sausage. It was traditionally made in November/December for consumption over Christmas and the New Year, and was a part of the picnics during winter shoots.

The name Collared Head is derived from the days before the general availability of large diameter casings. The Collared Head was made in a deep, wide tin, the top of which was weighted by all the irons in the house.

There are basically two types of casing. There is a plastic form that peels nicely off your salami. There is also a type that needs to be soaked. The latter does not peel easily but, as it is air permeable, the Collared Head matures better. Choose either, with a flat width of 4 to 8 inches.

3 half-pigheads
6 crubeens (pigs' feet)
6 hocks
2oz (60g) peppercorns (black or white)
$\frac{1}{2}$oz (15g) allspice
$\frac{1}{4}$oz (7g) cinnamon sticks
$\frac{1}{4}$oz (7g) mace blades
$\frac{1}{4}$oz (7g) cloves

Equipment

> A large bucket
> 3 to 4 pots, from 9 to 12+ pints
> Very sharp cutting knives
> Spice grinder
> Salami casing (for 15lb capacity)
> Sawn-off funnel
> Kitchen twine

An assistant is an advantage, and two pairs of wellies.

The pig must be cured in a strong pickle by a pork butcher for a minimum of 4 full days. Leave this to your butcher. Also, it is best to ensure that the heads are sawn rather than split.

Place the pig meat in the bucket and cover with water. Steep for 2 to 3 days, changing the water every morning.

Organised? Now here is your timetable: order the pig on Friday, collect it early on Wednesday, steep it until Saturday. Collared head is a weekend activity. You need the sharpest of knives, a bucket for bones and a pot for meat.

Prepare the heads by cutting off the ears. Put the ears and crubeens in a pot of water and simmer slowly for at least 3 hours. This will produce the jelly. Remove ears and crubeens, then with the sharpest knife in the house slice the ears as finely as you can. The crubeens are full of little bones, so be careful to remove them all.

Bring to the boil the hocks and half-heads in a different pot or pots, then simmer for 25 minutes. Take the pots off the heat and place as required on the kitchen table. Discard the water.

Take a piece of the pig, place on a cutting board, and strip the meat (which is not fully cooked) and other material from the bones. Then dice into ½in (1cm) cubes.

When working with the head do not include the eyeballs or any glandular material that may be revealed (it looks like mini-brains). Otherwise dice everything, with the understanding that the tougher it is, i.e. gristle, the finer you slice it. Put all the chopped meat (ears, crubeens, hocks and head meat) into a large pot.

Reduce the crubeen stock to about 7 to 8 pints (4l). When cool, this will set solid. Finely grind the spices. Thoroughly mix the freshly ground spices and stir into the pot of prepared meat. Add to this some of the reduced crubeen stock, slightly less than covers the meat. Simmer, while stirring, for not more than about 10 minutes.

Pour the meat mixture using a large jug through a 'sawn-off' funnel into the salami casings. Fill each casing to within two inches of the top. Tie with kitchen twine, just above the filled level, making a large loop, and proceed to the next casing. Be sure to stir the pot before taking another jug-full.

Hang up the 'salamis' in a cool place. By carefully rotating the end of the casing, you compress the sausage. Tie another tight noose to secure the compression. Mature them by hanging in an airy and very cool corner; alternatively, lay on the top shelf of a fridge. Of course, you might need to lie on the top shelf of a fridge yourself after trying this recipe. A gin and tonic is recommended as an alternative.

Note. The spice quantities are for a pre-boiled weight of 21lb (10kg) yielding a final weight of 15lb (7.5kg) of Collared Head. Slight adjustment may be necessary.

The question of too much pepper has been a point of annual discussion and hot debate at home for generations. The pepper quantities can be successfully reduced by up to two-thirds. White pepper was the original pepper used.
Makes fifteen lbs.

TRIPE AND ONIONS

The tall lady fell backwards among the plates of tripe.
'Two coffees and a collared head!' Maria announced emerging
from the kitchen before she saw the long drawn-out sweetness on
the tripe.
'The tripe and onions is off.'

Tumbling in the Hay

In the confusion of the Hay Hotel kitchen, while the medical students are curing Mércèdes who put her head in the gas oven, the porters are drinking tea and the coroner is eating tripe and onions, two acrobatic ladies compete on the table. Jenny Greeks, the circus lady, wins hands down, and the loser falls 'backwards among the plates of tripe'.

So, dear reader, we offer you two well-tested recipes for tripe, while confessing that tripe is really not our bag, and conclude that the balancing woman had a point when she squashed it off the menu.

    1lb (480g) tripe
    3 onions, sliced
    ¹/₂pt (300ml) milk
    1oz (30g) flour
    salt and pepper

Put the tripe, sliced onions and milk in a saucepan, cover and simmer gently for half an hour or until tender. Remove the tripe and place onto a hot dish, thicken the milk with the flour, season, pour it over the tripe and serve hot.
Serves four.

STUFFED TRIPE AND APPLE SAUCE

 1lb (480g) tripe
 ½lb (240g) boiled potatoes
 2 tbsp chopped cooked onion
 1 egg, beaten
 1 tsp dried sage
 1 tin chopped tomatoes

Put the tripe in a pot with cold water, bring it to the boil, cook for 5 minutes, lift out and discard the water. Cut the tripe into strips. Mix the other ingredients (except the tomatoes) to a stiff paste, put on the strips of tripe, roll them up and skewer them. Place in a casserole with the tomatoes and simmer gently for about 2 hours or until tender. Remove the skewers and serve with apple sauce.
Serves four.

Apple Sauce

 1lb (480g) cooking apples
 2 tbsp water
 ½oz (15g) butter
 juice of ½ lemon
 1oz (30g) sugar

Stew the apples very gently with the water and butter until soft. Beat them until smooth. Add the lemon juice and sugar.

PICNIC CHICKEN

'Come along' they were calling to each other when we signalled
that the feast was spread... 'And a little more chicken?'
As I Was Going Down Sackville Street

1 chicken (free range if possible. Chicken to be eaten cold needs plenty
   of flavour)
2 onions
bouquet garni
pinch of salt
6 green peppercorns
1 tsp paprika
3 sticks of celery

Put all the above ingredients in a pot and cover with cold water. Bring to the boil
and simmer gently for ³/₄ to 1 hour, depending on the size of the chicken. Remove
the chicken from the water and set it aside to cool. Then skin it and remove the
flesh from the bones. In the meantime, boil up the remaining stock and reduce it
to about ¹/₂ pt (300ml).

Sauce

1oz (30g) butter
1oz (30g) plain flour
¹/₂ pt (300ml) chicken stock
¹/₄ pt (150ml) cream
3 egg yolks, beaten
juice of 1 lemon
paprika

Melt the butter in a saucepan. Add the flour and cook gently. Add the chicken
stock. Stir until it boils, then let it cool slightly and add the remaining ingredients.
Stir until thick, without allowing it to boil. Season with a good dusting of paprika.
Half cool, then pour over the chicken.
Serves six.

CHAMPAGNE SALAD OF FRUITS

McGurk sat beside a Primus stove. Dr Tyrrell sat with his back to
a large stone on the top of which fruit salads were displayed. The
ladies fussed about with the dishes.

As I Was Going Down Sackville Street

This is an Edwardian recipe discovered by Fionn who initially approached it in
great trepidation only to discover that it is the reigning monarch of fruit salads — a
delight for the sensuously indulgent.

> 1 pineapple *or* 3 tiny pineapples
> 2 bananas
> 1 cantaloupe melon
> ½lb (240g) grapes
> ½lb (240g) black cherries
> ½lb (240g) strawberries
> 1 tbsp olive oil
> 1 tsp tarragon vinegar
> 1 tbsp sherry
> 1 tbsp of brandy
> sprig of fresh chervil
> sprig of fresh tarragon
> ½ pt (300ml) champagne
> 1oz (30g) pistachio nuts

Layer the fruit in a serving bowl, starting with the pineapple, then bananas, melon,
grapes, cherries, and strawberries on top. Mix the rest of the ingredients very well,
and pour over the fruit. Cover with cling film and leave in the refrigerator until
ready to serve.

Then pour over it a half pint (300ml) of champagne, and sprinkle with
pistachio nuts.
Serves eight.

WHISKEY PUNCH

'This is cold punch, Professor,' my wife said.
'Oh, indeed?'
'Now it is not a thing to be despised! The proportion of boiling water to 15 year old Jameson was, before it cooled, in exact ratio, to the amount of Falstaff's expenditure on bread as opposed to sack.'
'I cannot refuse.'

Gogarty gives us the perfect picnic, the picnic to crown all picnics, a scene from the Golden Age, before the First World War shattered everything. It was to celebrate his eldest son's fifth birthday and took place at Lough Dan in County Wicklow. The party included Professor Tyrrell, alias the Benign Doctor, and Professor Macran, also known as the Master of Those Who Know, Mrs Gogarty and her sister, the painter William Orpen and his cousin Alabaster, and the extraordinary Endymion, a famous Dublin eccentric. Orpen sketched the scene and the drawing was later cast in silver as a casing for the famous whiskey punch bottle, an Irish idyll immortalised. On a clear day you can still smell the whiskey!

    3 lemons
    1½ pt (900ml) boiling water
    8oz (240g) sugar
    1½ pt (900ml) whiskey

Peel the lemon rind very thinly, then squeeze the juice. Add to the boiling water and sugar. Dissolve the sugar. Then add the whiskey, strain the punch, and serve. It can be served hot or allowed to cool and bottled for picnics.

5

Seán O'Casey

Seán O'Casey, dramatist and socialist, was a child of the Dublin slums. Chronic ill-health and near blindness caused by malnutrition never dulled a voracious appetite for books. He was a manual labourer and secretary to the Irish Citizen Army when he first started to write, bewitched by Shakespeare and Boucicault. Lady Gregory encouraged him, and his first play *The Shadow of a Gunman* was produced by the Abbey Theatre in 1923. This was followed by *Juno and the Paycock* in 1924 and *The Plough and the Stars* in 1926. He wrote of the slums with passionate anger and created characters of mythic proportions: Fluther Good and Bessie Burgess, Captain Boyle and Joxer Daly. The Abbey's rejection of his play about the Great War, *The Silver Tassie*, confirmed his decision to remain in literary exile in England, where he wrote a further seven plays and six volumes of autobiography. He died in Torquay.

Seán O'Casey   1880 to 1964

> It was a simple Georgian house, one of a long terrace, with two
> decent rooms, a tiny bathroom, and a huge kitchen, with an old-
> fashioned range in it big enough to do as an altar for Stonehenge.
> And, by God, it burned the coal as fast as one could shovel it in,
> but took its time to heat the water. There was an oven in it would
> roast half an ox, my ox, your ox, his ox, her ox; but you would
> have to put a turkey into it on the very first of January if you
> wanted it cooked for Christmas.
>
> *Feathering His Nest: Autobiographies*

In *Rose and Crown*, Seán O'Casey describes setting up home for the first
time with his beautiful wife, the actress Eileen Carey. They had had a happy
honeymoon in Dublin, been driven far too fast by Oliver St John Gogarty,
stayed at the Russell Hotel and dined at Jammet's. O'Casey's very first
present to Eileen was a box of macaroons. They didn't have much money
but loved pictures and books, and Eileen brought some furniture from her
previous flat. This was just as well, for Seán's worldly goods he listed as 'two
pictures, a chair, a desk, kept together by the mercy of God, a cheap divan,
a crowd of books, a spoon, knife and fork, a kettle, tea pot and a few
articles of delfware.' Eileen didn't know how to cook when they were first
married, and the economics of shopping were a mystery. Seán could
manage to make wonderful tea and was a master of the perfectly boiled egg,
so that was what they ate most of the time, with the occasional foray to the
restaurant that had been their favourite place before they were married, the
Queen's Restaurant. Their Cockney daily couldn't cook either, and
produced inedible meals that were swimming in fat. It must have been a
relief to be invited to dine at the homes of their many friends in London.
They discovered too that the expenses involved in running a house were not
only in buying things for it (they rather liked Harrods and Heals) but also
in doing things to it. A new tank was needed, the roof was in a bad way and
the pipes needed replacing. No wonder O'Casey exclaimed, 'Jasus, it wasn't
half as easy as it had looked.'

Before their daughter Shivaun was born, the O'Caseys and their two
young sons, Breon and Niall, moved to Totnes in Devon, because George
Bernard Shaw had recommended Dartington Hall as the most desirable
school for the boys, and their parents did not want to be separated from
them. It was to prove a happy move — life in the country suited them all.
It was an ideal location during the War, when food was scarce and many
items were rationed; the farmers made sure Mrs O'Casey got her fresh fruit

and vegetables, chicken and eggs. Eggs were commonly referred to as 'breakables', so as not to divulge how many had been sold. And the consumption of 'breakables' was a vital part of the O'Casey diet. Every Sunday morning Seán prepared breakfast for his wife and children: tea, toast and perfectly boiled eggs served on trays and brought to them in their beds!

As a family the O'Caseys were a rarity in Dublin: poor and Protestant in a mainly Catholic city of such filth and disease that the infant mortality rate was higher than Calcutta. Seán O'Casey's mother set an example of faith and love. Seán and his mother were very close. He described the empty feeling in the house after his father's funeral; he, a little boy at the time, sitting with his grieving mother and watching the reflection of the fire in her tears. Her own death in 1918 shattered him. They had lived happily together for a long time and he was safe in her staunch protection of him. Eight babies had died before his birth and he was a sickly little thing from the start. His corneas were severely ulcerated, a side-effect of near starvation. His mother would not give up her fight for his eyes. She struggled, too, to give him a good education, but the death of her husband brought them to the poverty of tenement life that O'Casey presents in his plays. She was a woman of principle, and once when the hungry little boy took a small pinch of tea and sugar from a shop, she said:

Never do that again, Johnny. Remember what you have been taught: Take no thought for your life, what ye shall eat; not yet for your body, what he shall put on; for the life is more than meat, an' the body more than raiment.

As she lay dying she kept insisting that she would soon be better and able to look after him again. In *Mrs Casside takes a Holiday* he describes how he nursed her:

He got a small sack, and went to Murphy's, and carried back two stone of coal, bread, sugar, tea and a small jug of milk. Soon he had a good fire going, and when the kettle boiled, he filled the jar, wrapped it in an old torn shift, and carefully shoved it under the old bedclothes... He put the beef into a saucepan to stew; peeled the oranges; squeezed with the pressure of his hands as much juice as he could from them in a tumbler, adding some sugar and hot water.

Seán O'Casey had starved as a little boy on a diet of dry bread and tea. He described the rows of loaves in the bread van with the wistful nostalgia of a very hungry child, and the way the women queued at the milk van with their little jugs, only able to afford enough milk barely to dilute the strong black tea that they all drank so much. Eileen O'Casey told us that he never recovered his appetite as a result of the deprivations of childhood, and always ate very little during their life together. 'If I was not there to get him a meal, he would eat nothing. As for the small amounts he did eat, he liked fish and meat and ate most things.' His hunger for books was greater than his hunger for food, and when at last he was earning, he did without meals to indulge his appetite for words. He consumed Shakespeare and everything else he could buy from the book barrows along the quays on the River Liffey. He learned many of Shakespeare's plays by heart and maintained that nobody should dare write a play until Shakespeare was committed to memory. He was a builder's labourer until playwriting took over his life, and he was shy and terrified when his first play, *The Shadow of a Gunman,* was accepted for performance at the Abbey Theatre. One actor in the company said that he was no more than a reporter and that his play wouldn't last the decade.

The Abbey Theatre was formerly the old Mechanics' Institute, where, as a boy, O'Casey had received his first taste of the Irish dramatist Boucicault. When he returned as a playwright at the age of forty-three, he recalled a bizarre competition he had witnessed in his youth: a boiling hot suet-pudding eating contest with grown men, their hands tied behind their backs, competing for a ten-shilling prize.

His new profession had its social pitfalls, including an invitation to dinner at a famous restaurant 'with the elect people of Ireland in a ceremonious meal'. To Seán, the food wasn't good at all (except for the rhubarb and custard), and when Lennox Robinson asked him if he enjoyed his dinner, Seán replied with devastating truth which rather startled Mr Robinson:

What was there terrible in saying food was badly cooked? He based his remark on his mother's skill. Whenever she and he had had anything worthwhile, steak, mutton, liver or fish, garnished with vegetables, they were always sure to be handed up in a simple but first-class style of cooking. And all done on a plain open coal fire.

Missing his own mother, O'Casey had found a surrogate in his new, immensely kind champion, Lady Augusta Gregory, a founder of the Abbey along with W B Yeats and J M Synge. She was a dramatist herself, although far too much under Yeats's dark shadow in Seán's eyes. His first two plays,

The Shadow of a Gunman, and *Juno and the Paycock,* had saved the Abbey's reputation and its financial skin. The 'House Full' notice had to be put up for the first time in the Abbey's history. Both plays dealt with the hell of tenement living, but not in a didactic way; for O'Casey, it was the human personality that mattered. The slums are the backdrop for the creatures that populate the plays, sometimes predatory, often noble; he was unsentimental in the portrayal of the grim reality, relieved by a divine comic freedom. O'Casey's vision was essentially comic, shot through with tragedy, because that was the way he perceived life. In 1926, when O'Casey was forty-six, *The Plough and the Stars* shocked Dublin society and rocked its complacent foundation with its presentation of the three taboos of Irish convention: sex, religion and patriotism. The stories of these first performances have become theatre legend: punch-ups between performers and audience, the stage covered in chairs, shoes and vegetables, and best of all, W B Yeats at his grandest and most eloquent. Yeats's famous speech to the rioting audience acknowledged O'Casey's genius and recognised the riot as marking the dramatist's apotheosis. O'Casey was thrilled to hear of this, even if he did have to rush home to look it up in his dictionary!

Living a contented life with his family in England, O'Casey added eight more plays and six volumes of 'Autobiographies' to the *oeuvre,* as well as many articles and innumerable letters. Although nearly blind, he never stopped writing. With Shaw and Yeats, he was one of the 'indomitable Irishry'. His entire life was devoted to an impossible crusade, that of making the world a better place. Sometimes he appeared querulous (he rather liked the adjective 'waspish' applied to himself), but he was never ungenerous; his pen might have been filled with vitriol but there was no bitterness in the man that held it. More than anything else he was a joyous celebrant of life itself:

> *Here, with whitened hair, desires failing, strength ebbing out of him, with the sun gone down, and with only the serenity and the calm warning of the evening star left in him, he drank to life, to all it had been, to what it was, to what it would be. Hurrah!*

DUBLIN CODDLE

Boyle: Breakfast! Well, they can keep their breakfast for me. Not if they went down on their bended knees would I take it — I'll show them I've a little spirit left in me still! (He goes over to the press, takes out a plate and looks at it) Sassige! Well, let her keep her sassige. (He returns to the fire, takes up the teapot and gives a gentle shake. The tea's wet right enough.

Juno and the Paycock

Sausages of excellent quality are vital to make a good coddle. Coddle is indigenous to Dublin, and quite a few pubs serve it as a lunchtime dish. We are indebted to Biddy White Lennon, writer, food expert and fellow pig enthusiast, who gave us this recipe from her book *Traditional Irish Cooking* (Poolbeg), which we recommend.

> 3 large onions
> 3–4 potatoes
> a handful of freshly chopped parsley
> 1 lb (480g) bacon bits
> 1 lb (480g) good meaty sausages
> freshly ground black pepper

Peel and chop the onions roughly. Peel the potatoes as thinly as possible. If they are large, cut them into two or three pieces, otherwise leave them whole. Chop the parsley.

Place a layer of onions in the bottom of a heavy pot with a good close-fitting lid. Layer all the other ingredients, giving each layer a twist of freshly ground black pepper. Add no more than 2 cups of water to the pot. Bring the water to the boil, then reduce the heat at once, cover tightly, and barely simmer for 2 to 5 hours. The perfect way to cook it is in a heavy casserole pot in a very low oven at 120°C (250°F, Gas mark ½). The longer and slower the cooking, the better. If you prefer it, before serving, remove the sausages and quickly brown them on one side under the grill. Serve with white griddle bread to mop up the soup and bottles of stout. Serves six.

BROWN SCONES

There she and Johnny had a nice tea with homemade scones well warmed in the oven, melting in your mouth before you'd time to sink your teeth in them.

First the Green Blade

Scones are the backbone of afternoon tea in Ireland. They feature at teatime in nearly every novel that has a teatime in it, from Elizabeth Bowen to George Birmingham, from Somerville and Ross to the scrumptious teas in the garden described in Lady Augusta Gregory's *Journals*. They are best served warm, as Seán O'Casey remembers, so that the butter melts as you spread it. Don't forget the homemade jam.

12oz (360g) wholemeal flour
4oz (120g) white flour
1 tbsp wheatgerm
2oz (60g) castor sugar
1 level tsp bicarbonate of soda
1 level tsp cream of tartar
1 pinch salt
2oz butter
1 egg, beaten
½ pt (300ml) buttermilk

Preheat oven to 200°C (400°F, Gas mark 6).

Combine all the dry ingredients. Rub in the butter until it resembles breadcrumbs. Add the egg and buttermilk and mix well with a knife. Shape the dough into a round and flatten to ½in thickness. Cut out scone shapes with a 2½in (6cm) scone cutter, and place on greased baking tray. Brush the tops with a little milk. Bake for 15 minutes.
Makes approximately 20 scones.

WHITE SCONES

8oz (240g) plain flour
1 level tsp bicarbonate of soda
1 level tsp cream of tartar
1 pinch salt
2oz (60g) butter
2oz (60g) sugar
2oz (60g) sultanas
¼ pt (150ml) buttermilk

Preheat oven to 200°C (400°F, Gas mark 6).

Sift the flour with the bicarbonate of soda, cream of tartar and salt, and rub in the butter until it resembles breadcrumbs. Add sugar and sultanas and mix. Then add the buttermilk, mixing well with a knife. Knead lightly, shape the dough into a round and flatten to ½in thickness. Cut out with a 2½in (6cm) scone cutter, and place on greased baking tray. Brush the tops with a little milk. Bake for 15 minutes or until golden brown.
Makes approximately 10 scones.

WHITE SODA BREAD

> The carts were big and box-like, filled with double rows of shallow trays on which rested row after row of steaming loaves, tuppence or tuppence-farthing each... Underneath a deep deep drawer, going the whole length of the cart, filled with lovely white an' brown squares, soda squares, currant squares, and brown loaves, covered with their shining golden crust...
>
> *The Street Sings*

When Seán O'Casey was a little boy, tea and bread were his basic diet; no wonder his memories of the bread vans were so vivid, and was there ever money to buy the currant squares? The smell of freshly baked bread has to be one of the best smells in the world. We are self-confessed breadaholics, and if you want your kitchen to smell better than heaven, then follow these instructions:

    1lb (480g) plain white flour
    1 level tsp bicarbonate of soda
    1 level tsp cream of tartar
    pinch salt
    2oz (60g) butter
    4oz (120g) sugar
    2oz (60g) sultanas
    2oz (60g) raisins
    1 egg, beaten
    ½ pt (300ml) buttermilk

Preheat oven to 200°C (400°F, Gas mark 6).

In a bowl, sift the flour with the bicarbonate of soda, cream of tartar and salt, and rub in the butter until it resembles breadcrumbs. Add sugar and dried fruit and mix through. Add the egg and buttermilk, mixing well with a knife. Knead lightly and shape the dough into a round of about 3in thickness. Mark the top with a cross using a knife. Bake on a greased baking tray for 55 minutes or until golden brown—the base should sound hollow when tapped.
Makes one loaf.

BUNS

...and they often talked and laughed together over tea in a hotel
that overlooked the fair form of Stephen's Green; Seán trying to
look at home in the posh place, and succeeding in a way; she
eating bun after bun, murmuring that she was very, very hungry.

Where Wild Swans Nest

Seán O'Casey had a strong affection for Lady Gregory, whom he beatifies as
Blessed Bridget O'Coole in his autobiographical books. To him, she had a lovely
mixture of dignity and humour, and he considered her atrociously underrated by
her peers. He loved making gentle fun of her accent, with its slight lisp: 'Doh away,
woman; it's twite simple, and I tan handle it myself.' The same affection informs
the bun-eating episode; this unlikely couple were comfortable together, and what
better excuse could there be for a bun recipe?

This is the recipe our children like to use. They generally scoff them as soon as
they are out of the oven, but have been known to dress them up with instant icing
for friends.

> 1lb (480g) self-raising flour
> pinch of salt
> 5oz (150g) butter
> 2oz (60g) chopped candied peel
> 6oz (180g) currants
> 5oz (150g) sugar
> ¼ tsp ground nutmeg
> 2 eggs, beaten
> 2 tbsp milk

Preheat oven to 200°C (400°F, Gas mark 6).

Sift the flour and salt together. Rub in the butter until the mixture is like fine
breadcrumbs. Mix in the fruit, sugar and nutmeg. Add the egg and milk to the
flour mixture, mixing well with a fork. The dough should be very stiff; add more
flour if necessary. Divide into 24 pieces and form into rocky heaps on a greased
baking tray. Bake at 200°C (400°F, Gas mark 6) for 15 to 20 minutes.
Makes twenty-four buns.

LADY GREGORY'S BRACK

She usually brought one up for the actors when she visited Dublin. A lot of the actors and actresses elected to regard the cake with contempt, but they ate it all right, and when the tea was done, though the cake would feed a regiment, he had noticed that there was little left behind. The cake was a rich thing of spice, raisins, and currants, but the rarest thing in its make-up was a noggin of brandy to help to damp the dough.

Where Wild Swans Nest

Lady Gregory's Brack was a yeast brack, which is more complicated to make than a tea brack, so we offer you both recipes. The tea brack recipe belongs to Marion Doyle, Veronica's neighbour, and is guaranteed fool-proof; it's rather impressive as it's big and high. If you're not good at baking, this is the cake for you. This is not a reflection on Marion's baking talents, but probably is on Veronica's!

2 tsp honey
1oz (30g) fresh yeast *or* 1 tbsp dried yeast
1lb (480g) strong white flour
¼ pt (150ml) warm milk
¼ pt (150ml) warm brandy
2oz (60g) brown sugar
pinch of salt
1 tsp cinnamon
4oz (120g) currants
2oz (60g) mixed peel
4oz (120g) raisins
2oz (60g) butter
2 eggs, beaten
1 egg white, beaten
2oz (60g) icing sugar

Preheat oven to 175°C (350°F, Gas mark 4).

Mix together the honey, yeast and 4oz (120g) of the flour with the milk and brandy. Cover and set aside in a warm place until frothy (about 20 minutes). Sift together the flour, sugar, salt, cinnamon and fruit, and rub in the butter. Add the flour mixture and eggs to the yeast batter. Mix well to form a soft dough. Add extra flour if the dough is too sticky. Turn out on a floured board and knead until the dough is smooth and elastic. Oil the inside of the mixing bowl, return the dough to it, cover and leave to rise in a warm place until double in size. Then turn out and

knead again. Divide the dough in two and place in greased 8in (20cm) cake tins. Cover and leave to rise again. Bake for 50 minutes, until a skewer comes out clean. Then brush with beaten egg white (or milk), sprinkle with icing sugar and return to the oven for a few minutes until glazed. Stand them on their sides, and wrap in teatowels if you want a soft crust.
Makes two bracks.

TEA BRACK

Both bracks are usually eaten with butter.

> 1lb (480g) dried mixed fruit
> 8oz (240g) brown sugar
> 1 pt (600 ml) cold tea
> 1lb (480g) self-raising flour
> 1 heaped tsp mixed spice
> 2 eggs, beaten
> milk, if necessary

The night before you make the brack, place the fruit in a bowl with the brown sugar and pour the tea over it, mixing it so the sugar dissolves. Next day, preheat oven to 175°C (350°F, Gas mark 4). Sift the flour into a mixing bowl with the spice. Add the fruit mixture and the beaten eggs, mixing well and making sure there are no lumps of flour remaining. If the mixture seems very stiff, add a little milk. Place in a greased and lined 8in (20cm) cake tin and bake for 90 to 95 minutes. After the first hour, cover with a piece of brown paper so the top doesn't burn. Test it by inserting a skewer in the centre; if mixture still clings to it, bake for another 5 minutes.
Makes one brack.

RHUBARB TART

Seán was awakened out of the booming by the voice of Mr
Robinson asking him if he'd enjoyed the dinner, Seán dazedly
and innocently replying with The Rhubarb and Custard were
Fine, thanks, but the rest of the things were badly cooked; to be
startled by Mr Robinson ejaculating What a Terrible man you are
to bring to dinner!

Blessed Bridget O'Coole

Lennox Robinson was a playwright and became manager of the Abbey Theatre in
1919. He was a tall, wan and willowy man with a chronic drink problem. Oliver St
John Gogarty once remarked, on seeing him the worse for wear: 'Poached eyes on
ghost.' He can't have been unaware that Seán O'Casey was unused to restaurant
eating, but we think the O'Casey candour disarming.

        8oz (240g) plain white flour
        pinch of salt
        2 tsp castor sugar
        4 oz (120g) butter
        2-3 tbsp cold water
        4oz (120g) castor sugar
        1½lb (720g) rhubarb

Preheat oven to 200°C (400°F, Gas mark 6).

Sift and mix the flour, salt and 2 tsp sugar. Cut in the butter with a knife, then rub
in with the tips of your fingers. Add the water carefully, using as little as possible.
Press lightly into a ball of dough.

    Chop the rhubarb roughly into pieces about 1 inch long. Place in a 1½ pint pie
dish. Sprinkle 4oz (120g) sugar over the fruit. Line the edge of the dish with pastry
and cover the pie with pastry. Press the edges of the pastry with the back of a knife.
Brush the pastry with milk and sprinkle with brown sugar. Bake at 200°C (400°F,
Gas mark 6) for 10 minutes, then at 175°C (350°F, Gas mark 4) for 40 minutes.
Serve with thick cream.
Makes one tart.

6

James Joyce

James Joyce, poet, novelist, playwright and Ireland's most illustrious literary exile, was born in Dublin and educated there. In 1904 he met Nora Barnacle and left with her for Zurich, later living in Pola and Trieste, earning a precarious living as an English teacher. He never doubted his destiny as a great writer, but lack of money made life difficult until relief came from the Royal Literary Fund, then from Mrs McCormick, and most generously of all, from Harriet Weaver. *Dubliners*, a collection of superbly crafted short stories, was published in 1914. The *Portrait of the Artist As a Young Man*, published in the United States in 1916, states his creative intentions: 'I go to forge in the smithy of my soul the uncreated conscience of my race.' Sylvia Beach, owner of the bookshop Shakespeare and Company, published Joyce's masterpiece *Ulysses* in Paris in 1922. Despite chronic ill-health and an appalling eye condition, Joyce spent the next seventeen years writing *Finnegans Wake*. He predicted that its complexity would keep the critics busy forever. Joyce died in Zurich.

James Joyce   1882 to 1941

> We get out of bed at nine and Nora makes chocolate. At midday
> we have lunch which we (or rather she) buys (soup, meat,
> potatoes and something else)... At 4 o'clock we have chocolate
> and at 8 o'clock dinner which Nora cooks.
>> *Letter from James Joyce to his brother Stanislaus. 3 December 1904*

James Joyce loved food. But in the town of Pola, Nora had no stove, and
had to cook their food at the inn. In the nomadic existence of their thirty-
seven years together she never stopped longing for a proper home with a
proper kitchen. On 16 June 1904 (forever Bloomsday to all Joyceans) Joyce
met the red-headed chambermaid from Galway, who had the courage to go
with him on his odyssey of 'silence, exile and cunning'. The following
October they left Ireland, Joyce 'to forge in the smithy of my soul the
uncreated conscience of my race', Nora to face a life of hardship and
isolation, breaking the social conventions of her Catholic world, eloping in
secret without benefit of clergy.

Nora Barnacle was a good cook and, like Joyce, loved plain traditional
Irish fare, bacon and cabbage chased by lashings of hot tea; cakes and
puddings were her delight. She never lost her sense of fun, she never
understood the principles of home economics, and she never understood
her husband's work ('that chop suey' she called it on one occasion). She was
staunchly loyal, faithful, outspoken and down to earth. Nora was Joyce's
inspiration, his Lily, his Bertha, his Bella Cohen, his Molly Bloom; she was
also very funny.

The Joyces led a peripatetic existence (in their first two weeks in Trieste
they moved four times). They seemed to be in the habit of occupying bad
flats at good addresses in the cities of Trieste and Pola, Rome, Zurich and
Paris. They were continuously in a state of financial chaos and they were
often starving. When they had money they spent it. In a letter to his
brother Stanislaus, Joyce makes a food-inventory of a day out in the
country with Nora and their little son Giorgio:

10.30am	*Ham, bread and butter, coffee*
1.30pm	*Soup, roast lamb and potatoes, bread and wine*
4pm	*Beef stew, bread and wine*

6pm	*Roast veal, bread, gorgonzola cheese and wine*
8.30pm	*Roast veal, bread and grapes and vermouth*
9.30pm	*Veal cutlets, bread, salad, grapes and wine*

This epicurean blow-out occurred when Joyce was employed in a Roman bank. He also gave English lessons for a lira an hour but they could never earn enough money to satisfy their gargantuan appetites. He tried to impose economic sanctions on Nora. No more restaurants; tripe and onions in white sauce. Christmas 1906 found them completely moneyless and resigned to unadorned pasta for their dinner — an appalling state of affairs for a woman whose Christmas puddings were legendary; she would usually make four, and later in Trieste she had everyone chasing around the city searching for the right ingredients. Inanition spurred inspiration, for it was at this time that Joyce wrote 'The Dead', the last story of *Dubliners*, in which the Misses Morkan hold their annual dance at Christmas time ('they believed in eating well; diamond-bone sirloins, three-shilling tea and the best bottled stout'); the laden table is described in achingly lustful detail:

> *A fat brown goose lay at one end of the table, and at the other end, on a bed of creased paper strewn with sprigs of parsley, lay a great ham, stripped of its outer skin and peppered over with crust crumbs, a neat paper frill round its shin, and beside this was a round of spiced beef. Between these rival ends ran parallel lines of side-dishes: two little minsters of jelly, red and yellow; a shallow dish full of blocks of blancmange and red jam, a large green leaf-shaped dish with a stalk-shaped handle, on which lay bunches of purple raisins and peeled almonds, a companion dish on which lay a solid rectangle of Smyrna figs, a dish of custard topped with grated nutmeg, a small bowl full of chocolates and sweets wrapped in gold and silver papers and a glass vase in which stood some tall celery stalks. In the centre of the table there stood, as sentries to a fruit-stand which upheld a pyramid of oranges and American apples, two squat old-fashioned decanters of cut glass, one containing port and the other dark sherry.*

On 19 July 1920, the Joyce family arrived in Paris and began the familiar pattern of flat-hopping. 'We chase flats and are worn to exhaustion,' Joyce commented. Sylvia Beach, owner of the bookshop Shakespeare and Company, published *Ulysses* in 1922. This event, together with the patronage of the generous Miss Weaver, gave the Joyces financial security they had never experienced before.

Their various apartments, especially the last one at Rue des Vignes, are described as well-furnished and comfortable, though dark and heavily bourgeois. Joyce had an account at Fouquet's. At five o'clock every afternoon, tea was served with lots of cake. There were parties too though Nora always hated Joyce to get 'blithered', for he was a great consumer of white wine (red meat and red wine he wouldn't touch), and when in his cups liked to perform his celebrated spider dance. He loved Nora to cook for him and would buy special food that had happy associations for him. Chicken was her speciality and he liked to say, 'My wife used to cook over an open turf fire in Ireland'.

Ulysses describes the events of 16 June 1904 in Dublin. It begins with two breakfasts and lots of tea-making. In the tower at Sandycove, Stephen and Haines eat the fry and the bread and honey prepared by the 'mercurial Malachi':

> — *The blessings of God on you, Buck Mulligan cried, jumping up from his chair. Sit down. Pour out the tea there. The sugar is in the bag. Here, I can't go fumbling at the damned eggs. He hacked through the fry on the dish and slapped it out on three plates, saying:*
> - In nomine Patris et Filii et Spiritus Sancti.
> *Haines sat down to pour out the tea.*
> — *I'm giving you two lumps each, he said. But, I say, Mulligan, you do make strong tea, don't you?*
> *Buck Mulligan, hewing thick slices from the loaf, said in an old woman's wheedling voice:*
> — *When I makes tea I makes tea, as old mother Grogan said. And when I makes water I makes water.'*

Lunchtime finds Leopold Bloom reduced to nausea as he watches the men of Dublin at the trough:

> *Perched on high stools by the bar, hats shoved back, at the tables calling for more bread no charge, swilling, wolfing gobfuls of sloppy food, their eyes bulging, wiping wetted moustaches. .... A man with an infant's saucestained napkin tucked round him shovelled gurgling soup down his gullet. A man spitting back on his plate: halfmasticated gristle: no teeth to chewchewchew it. Chump chop from the grill. Bolting to get it over.*

No wonder Bloom opts for the cool of Davy Byrne's 'moral pub' and settles for a gorgonzola sandwich and a glass of wine:

Like a few olives too if they had them. Italian I prefer. Good glass of burgundy; take away that. Lubricate. A nice salad, cool as a cucumber. Tom Kernan can dress. Puts gusto into it. Pure olive oil. Milly served me that cutlet with a sprig of parsley. Take one Spanish onion. God made food, the devil the cooks.

The day ends with Stephen Dedalus sipping Epp's Cocoa in Bloom's kitchen. Upstairs Molly's sleepy reverie combines food and sex in a delicious concoction of female sensuality. She remembers a picnic on Killiney Hill when she was 'all stayed up', which made walking difficult, and 'the lovely teas we had together scrumptious currant scones and raspberry wafers I adore'.

Bloom is 'on the pop' of proposing marriage in the kitchen as she is rolling out potato cakes, up to her arms in flour. The first time she notices him she is eating; 'at dessert when I was cracking the nuts with my teeth I wished I could have picked every morsel of that chicken out of my fingers it was so tasty and browned and tender as any thing only for I didn't want to eat everything on my plate those fish forks and fish slices were hall-marked silver too I wish I had some I could easily have slipped a couple into my muff.'

James Joyce celebrated life in his work. Molly Bloom closes the most written about novel of the twentieth century with a multiple yes — sex and food, two of the pleasures of life:

Whatll I wear shall I wear a white rose or those fairy cakes in Liptons I love the smell of a rich big shop at 7¹/₂d a lb or the other ones with the cherries in them and the pinky sugar 11d a couple of lbs of course a nice plant for the middle of the table Id get that cheaper in wait wheres this I saw them not long ago I love flowers Id love to have the whole place swimming in roses God of heaven theres nothing like nature...the day I get him to propose to me yes first I gave him the bit of seedcake out of my mouth and it was leapyear like now Yes 16 years ago my God after that long kiss I near lost my breath yes he said I was a flower of the mountain yes...and then he asked me would I yes to say yes my mountain flower and first I put my arms around him yes and drew him down to me so he could feel my breasts all perfume yes and his heart was going like mad and yes I said yes I will Yes.

BLOOMSDAY BREAKFAST

Mr Leopold Bloom ate with relish the inner organs of beasts and fowls. He liked thick giblet soup, nutty gizzards, stuffed roast heart, liver slices fried with crustcrumbs, fried hencod's roes. Most of all he liked grilled mutton kidneys....

Ulysses

Read *Ulysses* and you can practically smell the kidney frying in butter and pepper and becoming a little singed (the cat gets the burnt bit — 'Mkgnao'). But the best breakfast in the book isn't even eaten by the man it's meant for — he faces imminent execution and with great magnanimity leaves his magnificent breakfast of rashers and eggs, steak and onions, hot rolls and tea to the Sick and Indigent Roomkeeper's Society!

This is not so much a recipe as a method of cooking a tasty breakfast for four people.

8 streaky rashers of bacon (smoked for more flavour)
4 lamb's kidneys
8 slices lamb's liver
2 eggs, beaten
4oz (120g) breadcrumbs *or* wheatgerm

The rashers are cooked first, as the bacon fat is used to cook the kidneys and liver. They should be fried gently so that the fat runs. When cooked to taste (some people like them very crisp), place on a hot plate in a warmed oven.

Kidneys next. If they are wrapped in suet, remove it, then slice in two and remove the core. They can be grilled or fried in the bacon fat. They cook quickly, 3 to 5 minutes, depending on the size. Place in the oven with the rashers.

The important consideration with liver is its texture, which should be smooth. If it is grainy, it is not good liver and will not taste right. Dip the liver slices first in the beaten egg, then roll them in the breadcrumbs (wheatgerm if you prefer). Fry them gently in the bacon fat for 3 to 5 minutes, depending on the thickness. Do not over-cook liver or it will be dry and tasteless.

You will probably have some beaten egg left over, so soak some slices of bread in it and fry quickly. Serve with bread, butter and tea.

ROAST GOOSE

> While Gabriel and Miss Daly exchanged plates of goose and
> plates of ham and spiced beef, Lily went from guest to guest with
> a dish of hot floury potatoes wrapped in a white napkin. This was
> Mary Jane's idea and she had also suggested apple sauce for the
> goose but Aunt Kate said that plain roast goose without any apple
> sauce had always been good enough for her and she hoped she
> might never eat worse.
>
> *Dubliners*

One of the traditional days for serving goose in Ireland was for dinner at Little
Christmas, the Feast of the Epiphany on 6 January. We have heard it called the
Women's Feast in some parts of rural Ireland because the men did the cooking —
we bet they didn't do the washing up!

Fionn and her family prefer a goose for Christmas because of its superior taste
compared to boring old turkey. And there's the added attraction of masses of
gorgeous goose fat, which just happens to make the most beautiful roast potatoes
in the world. There are all sorts of complicated theories on cooking your goose to
perfection, all fairly labour intensive.

The best goose Fionn's family ever had was the result of totally unaided
cooking, as they locked themselves out of the house one Christmas Day and it took
a couple of hours and a broken window before access to the goose was attained, by
which time the goose was perfect.

Potato Stuffing

>   2lb (1kg) potatoes
>   salt and pepper
>   3 tsp chopped sage
>   2 tsp chopped parsley
>   2oz (60g) butter, melted
>   2 small onions finely chopped
>   milk

Boil, drain and mash the potatoes, season well, add the herbs, melted butter and
onions. Moisten with a little milk if necessary.

Clean the goose and remove any lumps of fat; they can be rendered for
dripping. Stuff the goose with the potato stuffing and fasten it with a skewer. Prick
it all over to release the fat. Roast in a fairly hot oven, 190°C (375° F, Gas mark 5),
by placing it on the oven rack above the roasting tin (use a very deep roasting tin
because of the amount of fat). Allow for 20 minutes to the pound, plus 20

minutes. Cover the top of the bird with tin foil for 1 to 1½ hours to prevent it becoming too brown. The fat will run into the roasting tin below. This is then used for roasting the potatoes. Pour off excess fat and keep it because it is wonderful for frying. The potatoes should be parboiled and roasted underneath the goose for about 70 minutes before the goose is cooked. Remove the goose and turn up the heat; finish the potatoes until crisp and brown. Serve with apple sauce.
Serves four generously.

Apple Sauce

Stew 2 large peeled and chopped cooking apples in a saucepan with a cup of cold water, and a tablespoon of sugar if you have a sweet tooth.

SPICED BEEF

Spiced beef is pickled or salted brisket or round beef to which a spice mixture is added. The piece of meat is covered in a layer of spice which is well rubbed in. It is generally sold in vacuum packs to hold the spice mixture.

> 2–3lb (1–2½kg) spiced silverside of beef
> 1 chopped white turnip
> 2 sticks celery
> 1 chopped onion
> 1 diced carrot
> 2 bay leaves
> 2 tsp ground allspice

Put the meat in as small a saucepan as possible. Add the chopped vegetables, bay leaves and enough water to cover. Bring to the boil and simmer over a low heat until cooked: allow about half an hour per pound. When cooked, lift out, dust with allspice and leave to cool.

Spiced beef is eaten at Christmas, but in recent times it is readily available all year round, and can even be bought ready cooked in the supermarket.
Serves six.

STUFFED PORKSTEAK

Opposite Ruggy O'Donohoe's Master Patrick Aloysius Dignam, pawing the pound and a half of Mangan's, late Fehrenbach's, porksteaks he had been sent for, went along warm Wicklow Street dawdling.

Ulysses

In the chapter of *Ulysses* entitled 'Hades', we attend the 'funferall' of poor Paddy Dignam in Glasnevin Cemetery ('out of the frying pan of life into the fire of purgatory'). In 'Wandering Rocks' his son brings home the porksteak for the funeral party dinner that evening.

We have always thought of porksteak as a traditionally Irish cut of meat. Although it is not cheap, there is no fat or bone and it is truly delicious stuffed and roasted. In England it is referred to as pork tenderloin, but you don't see it displayed in butchers' windows with the same frequency as you do in Ireland. It was originally an old Viking favourite (a cut called a 'griskin', *griss* meaning a young pig in Old Norse), and what with Dublin's Viking heritage, who's to say that they did not introduce it to the Irish diet.

> 2 medium porksteaks
> 6oz (180g) beef dripping

Stuffing

> 1 onion, chopped
> 2oz (60g) butter
> 6oz (180g) breadcrumbs
> 1 tsp dried sage
> 2 sprigs fresh thyme
> handful of chopped fresh parsley

Preheat oven to 200°C (400°F, Gas mark 6).

Slit the porksteaks lengthwise to flatten them out but don't cut right through. Make the stuffing by gently frying the chopped onion in the melted butter until soft, and then adding the other ingredients. Heap the stuffing onto one porksteak and lay the other porksteak on top. Tie them together with string at 2in (5cm) intervals — usually three pieces of string are enough.

Melt the dripping in the roasting pan and place the meat in the centre. Arrange peeled potatoes around the edge. Cook in a hot oven for an hour and serve with apple sauce.

Serves six.

APPLE DUFF

> I might go over to the markets to see all the vegetables and
> cabbages and tomatoes and carrots and all kinds of splendid fruits
> all coming in lovely and fresh who knows whod be the first man
> Id meet theyre out looking for it in the morning...Id love a big
> juicy pear now to melt in your mouth
>
> *Ulysses*

Nora enjoyed making puddings. Brenda Maddox in her marvellous biography
describes a visit by the Joyces to their friends, the wealthy Baillys. Kathleen Bailly
was Nora's close friend, an Irishwoman living in France like herself, who also
enjoyed preparing good things to eat, even though she employed a cook in their
house outside Paris. Apples wrapped in pastry were a favourite dessert. This recipe
is for a film-editor we know who loves apples and pears.

4 dessert apples (Cox's orange pippins are best)
2oz (60g) brown sugar
2oz (60g) raisins
cinnamon to taste
1 beaten egg
½ pt (300 ml) cream, whipped
12oz (360g) pkt puff pastry, or as below

Pastry

6oz (180g) strong white flour
2oz (60g) wheatgerm
1 tsp salt
6oz (180g) butter
½ cup of cold water

Sieve the flour, add the wheatgerm and the salt. Mix well, then cut the butter in
with two knives until the pieces of butter are the same size as large peas. Add the
water and mix enough to moisten the ingredients. Turn out onto a floured board;
knead well, then roll out and use.

Preheat the oven to 200°C (400°F, Gas Mark 6).

Peel and core the apples. Stuff the centres with a mixture of brown sugar, raisins and cinnamon. Roll out the pastry and cut out 4 circles approximately 8in (20cm) in diameter, depending on the size of the apples. Place an apple in the centre of the pastry circle and brush the edge with beaten egg; draw up the pastry to enfold the apple, pressing the edges firmly to seal. Brush the tops of the pastry parcels with the remaining egg to glaze. Bake in a shallow ovenproof dish for 40 minutes. Serve with whipped cream.

Serves four.

COMFORTING BREAD PUDDING

> She made May collect the crusts and pieces of broken bread to
> help to make Tuesday's bread-pudding.
>
> *Dubliners*

The thought of using the breakfast leftover bread to make the pudding is not an appetising one. Bread puddings are somehow redolent of stodgy school meals and dining rooms reeking of yesterday's cabbage. In *The Boarding House* May is the maid in a rather grim boarding house, and that seems to fit the bread pudding image. Fionn's mother, however, has happier memories of this humble dish, and we are compelled to say that we were taken aback by the mouth-watering crunch of the bread contrasting with the creamy custard.

> 5 eggs, beaten
> 1 pt (600ml) milk
> 4oz (120g) sugar
> 14 slices of bread and butter
> 3oz (90g) raisins
> grated rind of ½ lemon

Preheat oven to 160°C (325°F, Gas mark 3).

Beat the eggs and add the milk and sugar. Line a 2½ pint ovenproof dish with one layer of buttered bread, with the corners pointing upwards around the sides. Sprinkle with ⅓ of the raisins and ⅓ of the lemon rind. Repeat until the dish is full. Pour in the egg and milk mixture and bake for 60 minutes.
Serves six.

DO BE CAREFUL TEACAKES

> Listen, here I'll wait on thee till Thingavalla with beautiful do be
> careful teacakes, more stueser flavoured than vanilla and
> blackcurrant there's a cure in.
>
> *Finnegans Wake*

Everyone's scared of reading *Finnegans Wake,* and those who have make sure
everyone else knows about it; it's like saying you've read all of Shakespeare's plays,
except that the Bard at least wrote English, even if it was a bit old-fashioned.
Finnegans Wake is a wonderful and rewarding book to dip into, especially if puns
and word play are your fancy. It is rich in culinary quips too. Who can resist a
book full of 'gourmandising and gourmeteering', offering such 'creative comforts'
to the palate as 'a cathedral of lovejelly', 'the peach of all piedom', 'vermincelly
vinagrette', or perhaps you'd prefer 'rat wi' fennel' and a 'box of biscums to the
jacobeaters', or 'whale's egg forced with pemmican'. All these munchables are
accompanied by edible jokes — 'King's royal college of sturgeons', 'one man's fish
and a dozen man's poissons', 'I had my billyfell of duckish delights', and even Mrs
Beeton is included in the credits, 'with them Murphy's puffs she dursted with
gnockmeggs and the bramborry cake for dour dorty dumpling obayre Mattom
Beetom'.

Late in life Nora said, 'What's all this about *Ulysses? Finnegans Wake.* That's the
important book.' Take Nora's word for it and give it a try, you might like it.

        1oz (30g) fresh yeast *or*
        ¹/₂oz (15g) dried yeast
        ¹/₄ pt (150ml) water
        1lb (480g) strong white flour
        1 tsp salt
        4oz (120g) castor sugar
        6oz (180g) melted butter
        ¹/₂ tsp grated nutmeg
        4 eggs, well beaten

Preheat oven to 200°C (400°F, Gas mark 6).

Mix yeast with the water and 1 teacup of the flour in a small bowl. Cover with a
clean cloth and leave in a warm place to form a sponge. Then add yeast mix to the

rest of the flour, salt and sugar. Add in the other ingredients; mix well and turn out on floured board and knead. Divide dough into 16 balls. Place them on baking trays and leave in a warm place covered with a damp cloth for 20 minutes to allow them to rise.

Brush with beaten egg before putting them into the oven. Bake for 20 minutes until nicely browned.

Eat hot, and do be careful not to drip the butter on your clothes and not to eat too many, or indigestion will ensue.

Makes 16 buns.

7

Kate O'Brien

Kate O'Brien, novelist and dramatist, was born into the Limerick merchant class. She chose the social milieu of her background as the setting for her novels. She was the first Irish writer to chronicle the rise of the wealthy Catholic bourgeoisie in Ireland. Her preoccupation was with women, their fetters and their freedom. Her books became best-sellers; *Without My Cloak* won the Hawthornden Prize and the James Tait Black Memorial Prize in 1931. Living outside Ireland gave her a detached outlook on Irish life. She thought of herself as essentially European. She died in Canterbury.

Kate O'Brien   1897 to 1974

> I may be a bit afraid of bossy waitresses, but I am not at their
> mercy. And I have tried, in quite expensive Irish hotels, to get my
> own way. I have asked, for instance, if I could have a minute
> steak, a plain green salad and a glass of wine. Always no. (I have
> asked everywhere.) I have asked for an apple or a pear at supper. I
> have asked for honey. I have been so driven in experiment as to
> ask if I could have a linen napkin instead of a paper one.
>
> *My Ireland*

Kate O'Brien had standards of excellence in food that singled her out as a
well-travelled woman in a country that was rather backward in its notions
of culinary expertise. When she was a little girl in Limerick, the food at
home was satisfying if plain, but her time at a boarding school run by the
French nuns at Laurel Hill introduced her to a distinctive way of eating —
the French way, which opened her eyes to all sorts of possibilities outside
her native land. She was a student at University College Dublin during the
desolate 1916-19 years and became a staunch Francophile, confident that
anything bearing the French label, be it food, wine or literature, was simply
a matter of perfection. In 1923 she went to Spain to work as a governess, an
Irish Miss, and there began a great love affair with that country, which was
to provide the setting for two of her novels, *Mary Lavelle* and *That Lady*.
Later in London, journalism, play writing and novel writing followed with
marked success, but the writer never lost her addiction to travel.

Kate O'Brien used to say that she loved Ireland with a 'fidgety' kind of
love, but this did not prevent her from voicing criticism at the low
standards in the quality of food and its presentation in Irish hotels and
restaurants.

Her last book, *My Ireland*, was a highly personal traveller's account of
Ireland. Her joy and pride in the country of her birth is undisputed, but
she resented the appalling food that seemed to be *de rigueur*. One of her
personal hates was what she called the 'big fry':

> *That fearful meal, of which the whole hotel reeks between the hours of six
> and seven-thirty... the crowded platter of fried meats, the dull triangles of
> toast always of the same bread and cut the same way, the strong tea (which is
> the best of the awful spread) and the truly scandalous, cheap jam.*

It worried her that Ireland, which was just beginning to work hard at its tourism industry and was becoming aware of the special qualities that made it such a desirable playground, should be so obsessed with the adjective 'luxury', but seemingly unable to understand the importance of good food:

> *I am speaking what I know — and I know it for all the country, from Antrim to Cork, from Derry to Waterford. I have suffered this fearful kind of supper in hotels that assuredly could and should do better, and I blame them not only for the charges they make for loathsome meals, but because their slovenly insolence drags Ireland back, keeps her dull.*

Kate O'Brien took her childhood world of solid comfort, Victorian furniture, Benediction and Mass, card parties and tennis, music and large Sunday dinners, and made of it the basic material of her creative imagination. Her first novel, *Without my Cloak*, which became a best seller, bears the hallmarks of her work in its emotional intensity, its narrative skill and its extraordinarily vivid detail. It is also the only one of her novels to have anything like a happy ending. Affairs of the heart in Kate O'Brien's writing end in tears. The saga of the Considine family spans the period 1860-77 and tells the story of the loves and relationships of this emotional, voluble and close family, whose name is held with pride and a reputation that must be protected at any cost. When Anthony Considine finishes building an ostentatious and rather ugly home outside Mellick, the entire family is invited to Sunday lunch of soup, the first roast lamb of the season, and apple tart. All Considine parties are 'cushioned with cream', Anthony's son's birthday party in June is 'mountained with strawberries', and a buffet party which reflects the family's wealth and social status is of epic proportions:

> *Cold fowl, cold game, cold ham, salmon mayonnaise, lobster salads, cucumber salads, sandwiches, olives, salted almonds, petits fours, eclairs, cherry flans, fruit salads, the famous Considine trifles. Coffee-pots and tea-pots of old Dublin silver. Jugs after jugs of cream. Rows of bottles, rows of decanters, Moselle cup sparkling through Waterford glass.*

It is a scandal of enormous proportions when Caroline, no longer able to bear a loveless marriage, runs away to London to seek the understanding of her favourite brother Eddy, and there falls in love. But her 'harsh traditions of honour and fidelity' and the outrage of the family, personified by her brother Anthony, bring her back to Mellick. Before she leaves London the urbane Eddy treats her to a wonderful dinner at Brown's Hotel:

They ate a fantastic supper, the kind they loved, as expensive and out-of-season as could be. Mushrooms, plover's eggs, langoustes... A remarkable supper, and no doubt the waiters thought they were celebrating a remarkable event — as indeed they were. It isn't every day that an Irish wife picks up her skirt and runs for it.'

Kate O'Brien fled to Spain in 1923 in order to evade marriage. The following year she married a Dutchman, Gustav Renier, but it lasted only eleven months, before she left, pleading an incompatibility of temperaments. She chose to live in London during the war, just as she chose to live in Connemara in the fifties. In 1961 she returned to England, where she lived until her death.

In *The Last of Summer*, Irish food seems to be granted a reprieve as a succession of delicious meals are consumed by the Kernahan family, all made up of the nicest of summer produce — cold roast chickens and ducklings, 'very fine salads' and fruit, superb homemade breads and apple-pie. Tom Kernahan falls in love with his French cousin Angèle, but their relationship is coldly and efficiently destroyed by his mother, a tough, utterly selfish and unscrupulous character. There is a marvellously memorable picnic on the dizzy heights of the Cliffs of Moher; an atmosphere of fun and high spirits as Angèle is introduced to the exhilarating delights of County Clare, scene of Kate O'Brien's happy childhood holidays. They eat masses of lobster mayonnaise, washed down by hock cup and followed by fruit and unsurpassable jam puffs.

One of the endearing discoveries in Kate O'Brien's novels is the plethora of delicious drinks she describes; her characters drink Charles Heidsieck champagne in Ireland, Pol Roger in London, the Frascati and Capri wines in Italy, hock, Moselle and of course the native porter of Ireland, with the odd gin and tonic thrown in.

There is an innocence and naïvety in the heroine's enjoyment of the food and wine in *As Music and Splendour*, which is in contrast to the sophisticated meal Clare eats with Iago Duarte, her mentor, when her first real success as Alceste is greeted with acclaim by the opera-going Neapolitans. Duarte promises her a Lucullan feast, although her preferences, true to her origins, are for a chop and floury potatoes. In an idyllic scene in a restaurant in a rose garden above the sea, there is a celebratory feast:

A young waiter had filled their glasses with green-gold Capri. Another boy was serving Clare's plate from a smoking dish of aubergines and shrimps.

To Clare, used to the simplicities of omelettes and fresh fruit, the food appears excessive:

> *Small red mullet — 'the little salmonetes of Spain' said Iago, 'and never perfect unless caught and cooked at once off the Viscayan coast. The salmonete is not a Mediterranean fish. Very few good fish are, you know—'*
> *'This Mediterranean fish is good enough for me,' said Clare. 'I didn't know you were a gourmet, Iago?'*
> *'My God, I'm not!'*
> *'I find them bores, the few I've met.'*

Like all O'Brien heroines, Rose and Clare learn that the price of love is pain, with the grim experience of loss and the inevitable tears.

Fanny in *The Flower of May* is prevented by rather selfish parents from completing her education in Brussels, on the assumption that she will eventually marry, so academic success is superfluous. Like Anna in *The Land of Spices* she is saved from the life of a dependant by an older woman, in Anna's case the English Mother Superior at her convent school, in Fanny's case, her aunt. Before this chance of liberation is offered to her, Fanny travels to Brussels to stay with her closest friend Lucille de Mellin and to accompany her family to Venice. Before she leaves, she meets Lucille's brother André-Marie, who is a cad of the first water, but a true gourmet, who finds the 'sad mutton' and 'the pudding of rice' — characteristic of the Irish hotel menu — understandably quite grotesque. His mother, the Countess, a lovely and erratic character, cannot understand a country that does not eat in a civilised manner; the food in her house is exquisite, and she worries that her pale little Irish guest has no appetite:

> *You saw for yourself that she didn't touch her duckling, or the really perfect artichokes, or the salad. And — can you remember? — did she or did she not eat the rum omelette? I believe she enjoyed the cherries, which are delightful just now. But what are a few cherries, if you haven't eaten your dinner?... The Irish seem to eat — very peculiarly. André-Marie says that their food is positively extraordinary.*

André-Marie eventually gets his deserved come-uppance from Fanny when, with a light touch of blackmail, she banishes him from Ireland. She discovers the value and power of freedom: 'But I was free — and I could kiss you, and leave you', and she does.

In 1950 Kate O'Brien bought what she called a Victorian villa, The

Fort, in Roundstone, Connemara. She lived there with her much-loved cats for eleven years. The locals admired her daring, for the house was known to be haunted and, legend had it, overrun by fairies. However, Miss O'Brien made no complaints about sleeping there until a particularly chilly autumn caused an invasion of mice which she mentioned to the butcher:

> *'Mice, did you say? Below in the house?'*
> *I nodded.*
> *He trimmed a chop with care, and threw a piece to his dog, Moscow.*
> *'Mice!', he said. 'so that's it! So they're coming in to you in the form of mice!'*

In the face of such incontrovertible wit and Irish charm, Kate O'Brien could only forgive her countrymen for not feeding her properly. There is a great and forgiving warmth in the memory of a welcoming breakfast one cold, black morning when stranded in Waterford, and the hospitable woman who served it:

> *an ageing, conventional figure in black and white who whisked round a high service screen bringing miracles of comfort to us at the speed of light. Tea to this poor gentlemen; coffee to you, sir, God help you. Tea for you, miss — and gladly I scalded myself with it. Bacon for you, sir; chops, is it, sir? Toast, butter, brown, rough bread — she flew about. And what for you, miss, as she rushed some toast at me.*
> *'Oh nothing', said I. 'This is marvellous, this is all.'*

PARMESAN CHEESE SOUFFLÉ

Idiotic, how-are-you, Sir! And I with a cheese soufflé, no less to place before ye! Come on here, Miss Eleanor, and let you whip it on to the plates before it's destroyed! I think it's out of her mind Mrs Hession is going, with her soufflés, I thank you!

The Flower of May

Soufflés are reputed to be difficult because of their sinking propensities, but Fionn says she's never had a failure with this recipe. It's easy to make and always impresses the guests. Served with a good mixed salad, it is popular for either lunch or supper.

> 2¹/₂oz (75g) plain flour
> 1oz (30g) ground rice
> 3¹/₂oz (100g) butter
> 3 egg yolks
> pinch paprika and salt
> 1 pt (600ml) milk
> 6oz (180g) Parmesan cheese, grated
> 6 egg whites, stiffly beaten, with a pinch of salt
> 1oz (30g) butter, cut into small pieces
> ¹/₂oz (15g) butter, to grease the dish

Preheat the oven to 175°C (350°F, Gas mark 4).

Butter a 2¹/₂ pint soufflé dish. Put the flour, rice, butter, yolks of eggs, paprika and salt in a heavy saucepan. Mix well, then stir in the pint of milk. Continue to stir over a gentle heat until it boils and thickens. Remove from the heat. Beat well to make sure the mixture is smooth. Fold in the Parmesan cheese and then the egg whites. Pour the mixture into the soufflé dish, and dot the top with little pieces of butter. Bake for ³/₄ hour at 175°C, 350° F, Gas mark 4.
Serves six.

HAM

Grandfather, the cats fed, at last gave Fanny a plate of beautifully carved ham. There was salad too, and the potato cakes, blazing hot in a silver dish on wheels with a spirit-lamp under it.

The Flower of May

No one really knows exactly why Limerick ham had such a world-wide reputation for excellence, a reputation which began in the middle of the last century and travelled the British Empire. There were three important bacon factories in Limerick: O'Mara's on Roches Street belonged to the family that Veronica married into, and was founded by James O'Mara in 1839. Kate O'Brien's sister Nance married Stephen O'Mara, whom she describes in *Presentation Parlor* most flatteringly. Miss O'Brien went to the United States as James O'Mara's secretary in 1922 when he was raising money for de Valera there. Veronica's father-in-law is truly knowledgeable on the subject of ham. The label on O'Mara products used to boast 'Best in the World', a claim not without foundation as the O'Maras opened a factory in Russia in 1891 and had offices in Romania and London.

Stephen O'Mara, senior, says you must always steep the ham overnight in cold water. It is a different cut nowadays to the ones he remembers in his youth; then the ham was cut in a semi-circle up into the back of the pig and included the gammon rashers. If you cook a shank of ham (a more economical cut) you know when it's cooked by the easy removal of the little bone called the mustard spoon (in the shank). Skin it and cover with breadcrumbs before carving.

> 3lb (1½ - 2kg) pale or smoked ham
> water
> 1 lemon, cut in quarters
> 2 bay leaves
> parsley
> 2oz (60g) brown sugar
> whole cloves

Put the ham in a large saucepan and add water until it reaches the top of the ham. Bring to the boil, then drain off all the water and remove any scum that has formed. Fill the saucepan up with water again and add the lemon, bay leaves and parsley. Bring to the boil and simmer for 20 minutes to the pound, plus 20 minutes.

When it is cooked remove the skin and score the fat with a sharp knife, making a criss-cross pattern; press brown sugar all over the fat, with cloves stuck in at intervals.

Serves six generously.

LOBSTER MAYONNAISE

'You're a brave man for your age, Corney,' said the Doctor.
'Lobster mayonnaise, and potato salad and far too much of this
very fresh bread! And as for your hock cup — you ought to be
shot, man! It's a terror!' Corney chuckled.'

The Last of Summer

Family picnics are so often of the peanut butter and packet of crisps variety.
Sometimes, however, an effort on a grander scale is called for, and cold lobster in
homemade mayonnaise served with brown bread, potato salad and a chilled bottle
of Entre Deux Mers is extravagant and elegant.

2 cold cooked lobsters
2 large fresh lettuces
10 tarragon leaves
1 sprig or ½ tsp dried chervil
4 scallions (spring onions)
½ pt (300ml) mayonnaise

Put the lobsters into a large pot of cold, salted water and gradually bring to the boil.
Keep boiling for 20 to 30 minutes, depending on their size.

Wash the lettuce and arrange on a large plate. Chop the herbs and scallions and
sprinkle over the lettuce. Cut the lobster in half lengthways, scoop out the meat
from the body, mix with a little mayonnaise, and return. Remove the meat from the
tail, slice it and arrange it in overlapping slices with the red side up. Arrange the
lobster on the bed of lettuce and garnish with the claws.
Serves two.

Mayonnaise

2 egg yolks   salt and pepper
2 tbsp white wine vinegar   ½ pt (300 ml) olive oil
¼ tsp English mustard   1 tsp hot water

Put the yolks, vinegar, mustard and seasoning in the food processor. Whisk to a
froth. With the machine still on, add the oil in a slow trickle. Then add the hot
water. Adjust the seasoning to taste.

Lobster needs a good, eggy mayonnaise, so don't be tempted to add the
eggwhites.

TROUT WITH FENNEL SAUCE

'Such trout I haven't eaten in a lifetime, Una!'
'Liam caught them. Indeed, if I'd remembered that I'd have let
him sit up and watch us eat them. Be sure to tell him tomorrow
that they were absolutely delicious.'
'The dapping is good this year,' said Will.
'You'll come on the lake tomorrow, won't you?'
'You're just in time for the last of the mayfly.'

Pray for the Wanderer

Trout is one of the great classic fish dishes of Ireland; it has a nostalgic flavour,
hinting at summer memories, evenings on the rivers, sunsets and being bitten to
death by midges. With the advent of fish farms both brown trout and sea trout are
now available all the year round. It doesn't do to be too exclusive about farmed
fish. A fresh farmed trout is still much nicer that a long-dead wild one. The trout
can also claim to be a literary fish: Oliver St John Gogarty wrote a poem called
'The Trout', and in W B Yeats's 'The Song of Wandering Aengus', the little trout
is transformed into a beautiful gleaming girl.

4 brown trout	2 tbsp sunflower oil
salt and pepper	

Preheat oven to 200°C (400°F, Gas mark 6).

Trout is best very fresh and plainly cooked, otherwise it is inclined to lose its
delicate flavour. Scrape the scales off with the back of a knife; cut off the fins, gut
and rinse the fish in cold water. Pat them dry, then cut sideways slits along each
side, about 1/2in apart. Season the fish with salt and pepper and oil. Put them in a
baking tin and add a tablespoon of oil. Bake in the oven for about 15 minutes.

Fennel Sauce

Take a handful of green fennel fronds. Wash well and pick the little sprigs from the
stalks.

1oz (30g) butter	4 tbsp cream
2 egg yolks	1 1/2 tbsp white tarragon vinegar
salt and pepper	

Put everything except the fennel in a saucepan over a bain-marie and stir until
thick. Remove from the heat, stir in the fennel and serve with the fish.
Serves four.

DUCKLING WITH WALNUT STUFFING

> They ate roast ducklings in the Carlton. Eddy, as he sipped his
> wine, looked gravely into Caroline's eyes and was assured that she
> was having some of the great-fun-in-spite-of-everything that he
> had promised her.
>
> *Without my Cloak*

Fionn and Veronica remember attending a dinner party where everything was
perfect except for the fact that there were two ducklings for eight people! The ratio
really is two people to one duckling. It is the most palatable of fowl if the skin is
crisp and the fat well drained. To achieve this effect, the duckling should be roasted
upsidedown on the oven rack above the roasting tray. Not much fun for the ducks
we suppose, but the Irish will do anything for the quack!

Walnut stuffing

> 2 tbsp sunflower oil
> 1 onion, chopped
> 4oz (120g) walnuts, chopped
> 1 tbsp parsley, chopped
> 1 tbsp thyme, chopped
> 1 tsp marjoram, chopped
> 4oz (120g) breadcrumbs
> 1 egg, beaten
> salt and pepper
> juice of ½ lemon
>
> 1 duckling
> 1oz (30g) butter
> ½ pt (300 ml) of chicken stock
> 1 glass red wine
> 4 tbsp honey
> 1 tsp arrowroot
> 2 tbsp blackcurrant jam

Heat the oil and fry the onion and walnuts gently, until the onion is soft. Turn into
bowl and mix in the rest of the ingredients. The chopped liver of the duck may also
be added.

Preheat the oven to 190°C (375°F, Gas mark 5). Stuff the duck, prick it all over and then rub over with the butter. Roast the duck, breast-side down, on a rack above a baking dish for ³/₄ hour at 375°F. Then remove the baking dish, drain off the fat, pour in the stock and wine, and replace in the oven. Turn the duck breast-side up and pour the honey over it. Roast for a further ³/₄ hour at 375°F, basting at intervals. This method ensures that the breast is not overdone and that most of the fat is drained off. Make the gravy by pouring the stock into a saucepan. To thicken, slake the arrowroot in a little red wine, then add to the stock and bring to the boil. Season with salt and pepper and add the blackcurrant jam. This gravy should be thin, so, if necessary, add more stock or wine.
Serves two.

AN IRISH SUNDAY DINNER

The very next Sunday all the family came over to River Hill to eat roast lamb and rhubarb tart, and for the deeper purpose of behaving to Caroline as if she had not just given them all the fright of their lives.

Without my Cloak

The tradition of Sunday dinner in Ireland is still upheld in many families. It is usually eaten in the middle of the day and should consist of a roasted joint of meat, with gravy and roast potatoes, one or two vegetables, and a dessert of apple tart with lots of cream. In both our houses, the Sunday dinner is considered a good opportunity to have the entire family in one place at the same time; to sit down and eat and talk in a hopefully civilised manner.

Veronica's husband Stephen has a theory based on the simple tenet that the entire production of Sunday dinner revolves around the roasting of potatoes. Kate O'Brien would possibly agree, as Sunday dinners have a place of importance in her novels; occasions where entire families can be observed, and in *Without my Cloak* she mentions the marvellous smell of roast potatoes being cooked and sold in the streets of Mellick. Somerville and Ross stated that there were two important things in Irish life: potatoes and hounds.

Different varieties of potatoes lend themselves to different cooking methods. Golden Wonders are perfect for roast, as they become crispy on the outside with a nice, floury inside. They must be cooked in dripping (fat that has been collected over a period of roast dinners and stored in the fridge) in a pre-heated oven in a roasting dish, with the meat in the centre. If the joint is larger than 3lb, then that must be put in on its own first. They will take 1 hour to 1 hour 20 minutes to achieve the golden brown effect, in an oven at 220°C (425°F, Gas mark 7), and must be turned over and basted half way through.

When you have transferred the meat and the potatoes onto serving dishes and put them in the oven, it is time to make the gravy on the roasting pan. Dinner should be served as soon as the gravy is ready, otherwise the potatoes will be like hotel ones, which are horrid.

8

Elizabeth Bowen

Elizabeth Bowen, novelist, was born in Dublin to an Anglo-Irish family. She was always conscious of her place in that class and tradition and described herself as an Irish novelist before all else. She had a special affinity with Bowen's Court, the family home in County Cork. Her first book of short stories came out in 1923, followed by the novel *The Hotel* in 1927, and then *The Last September*, which describes life in the Big House in County Cork. Her stay in London during the Blitz was the most exciting time of her life and inspired *The Heat of the Day*, which she considered her best work. An impeccable stylist, her literary preoccupation was 'life attenuated to the snapping-point', a mixture of the sophisticated and the sensual. Elizabeth Bowen died in London.

Elizabeth Bowen 1899 to 1973

> Mrs Vermont ate more hot cakes than she cared to remember because they were so good and nobody seemed to notice. She went on to chocolate cake, then to orange layer cake, to which she returned again and again. An idea she had had, that one should not eat very much when invited out, languished; she finished up with a plate of raspberries.
>
> *The Last September*

Elizabeth Bowen was rather keen on good manners and treats Mrs Vermont, a British officer's wife of dubious social standing and vulgar ways, with no mercy, at the same time enjoying the humour of the situation. Afternoon teas, delicious or grim, happen constantly in Elizabeth Bowen's novels and short stories; they provide neat opportunities for revealing her characters' thoughts and feelings, their interaction with each other and for amusing us. Life for Elizabeth Bowen was infinitely amusing, and she considered it one of the purposes of her books to be entertaining.

Elizabeth Bowen's mother did not care for shy children so her daughter, an only child, was encouraged to be sociable and to give and attend parties in the Protestant and upperclass Dublin of her birth. Her early life was divided between the Georgian terraced house at Herbert Place in Dublin and Bowen's Court, the family home in County Cork, a Big House in the Anglo-Irish tradition, a home that Elizabeth loved deeply and which gave her the blueprint for the country houses of her fiction.

When first married she moved to Oxford and began to lead the social life she loved, a round of dinners and parties that depended for their success on the brilliant conversational powers of the guests. Oxford was the setting for an extraordinary crowd at that time, and Bowen became one of them, a set that included Cyril Connolly, Cecil Day Lewis, Maurice Bowra, John Betjeman and Evelyn Waugh, Anthony Powell and A J Ayer.

Her talent for entertaining developed further when they moved to London, where her husband worked for the BBC. The house on Clarence Terrace near Regent's Park became the setting for an endless round of afternoon teas, drinks and dinners. Her wide company of friends had an eclectic quality — writers, friends and critics brought spouses, lovers and more friends. Lady Ottoline Morell, the elderly queen of London society, even suggested that she was handing over her mantle as the hostess who most mattered, to Elizabeth. The Bowen salon continued right through the war, even when food and alcohol were difficult to acquire, and Elizabeth only liked the best. There is a story of her wheedling an enormous veal and ham pie out of a restaurant one lunch time so that she could serve it to her dinner guests that night.

In Bowen's Court, as an adult, Elizabeth hosted wonderful house parties; the price of food and wine was never considered and she spent money excessively perhaps, but mostly for the purpose of keeping the Big House going and filling it with amusing and friendly people every summer. After dinner each evening, games were played in the Long Room, a sort of empty gallery which was the heart of the house. These games might be physical or cerebral (in her seventies Elizabeth Bowen had the killer instinct as a Scrabble addict). One game involved everyone composing the most disgusting dinner menu possible, with drinks.

Molly Keane remembers those parties with delight; she always thought the American and British guests very odd, however, in their complaints about the plumbing and there being only one bathroom, but she was used to Big House living. She also remembers Elizabeth's cook, Molly O'Brien, who began at Bowen's Court in 1927 and who cooked the most marvellous food. Elizabeth Bowen had no leaning towards the domestic side of things and did not cook, but then, few women of her class did; however, she had a fine appreciation for the pleasures of the palate. The garrulous side of her nature seems to belong to the 'flaithiúlacht', or excessive generosity of traditional Irish hospitality.

Bowen's Court is the Danielstown of *The Last September*, Bowen's second novel, in which she presents us with the familiar Bowen characters: the young girl, Lois, on the brink of womanhood and love, and the interfering older woman. The novel powerfully evokes that period in Ireland in the twenties when the old order was collapsing, and violence, murder and house-burning were the common currency. One of the hallmarks of the Anglo-Irish was the value they put on courtesy, and it is by way of their faultless good manners that the gentry deal with an impossible situation. The local people, held in affection, are nevertheless potential enemies, the British army is of dubious assistance, and their own ambivalent attitudes to their country emerge. Elizabeth Bowen was very conscious of her place in the Anglo-Irish tradition. 'I regard myself as an Irish novelist,' she said. Her comic vision, always an integral part of her unique style, owed much to Maria Edgeworth and Somerville and Ross. Bowen's subject is 'life with the lid on', a hot house of developing feelings and apprehensions, with the increasingly unbearable sensation that something disastrous is about to happen. Passion and terror are always under the surface, the louche, the sensational, lurks beneath, and what Bowen calls 'life attenuated to the snapping point' is a characteristic of all her work.

The heart-breaking situation in Ireland is not without humour, for if Bowen's work is a comedy of manners, then *The Last September* is a comedy of good manners as upperclass Irish country society deals with the vulgar wives of English officers. The enacting of tragedy is felt and even presaged in the burning orange of the evening skies, but the inexorable round of tennis parties, afternoon teas and dinners must continue because that is how one holds on. The English officers, especially the unmarried ones, are welcome as there is a shortage of suitable men because of the Great War, but the wives are not. At the tennis party where Mrs Vermont makes such a glutton of herself, the Irish and English attitudes are examined amusingly:

> *'Your scrumptious Irish teas make a perfect piggy-wig of me. And dining-room tea, of course, makes me a kiddy again!'*
> *'Does it really?' said Mrs Carey, and helped herself placidly to another slice of the chocolate cake. She thought of Mrs Vermont as 'a little person' and feared she detected in her a tendency, common to most English people, to talk about her inside.*

Mrs Vermont goes on to commit the social gaffe of introducing Irish politics at the tea party, a subject permissible among their own sort, to each other, but not with English outsiders. She manages to clear the table of guests by telling them that they, the English army, are in Ireland to take care of their hosts.

Lady Naylor, mistress of Danielstown and Lois's aunt, thinks of English servants as stupid and inhuman. Her relationship with her cook is interesting:

> *Kathleen, the cook, who resembled her mistress in personality so closely that their relation was an affair of balance, who had more penetration than Lady Naylor and was equally dominant.*

The cook, realising that there is an unsuitable romance between Lois and an English officer named Gerald, suggests slapping up a Sally Lunn cake for tea, as Gerald is expected. Lady Naylor thinks drop-cakes more appropriate, so confirming Kathleen's opinion of the situation. Her reaction is to send up for tea 'an unaccountable iced cake, ironically festive' for she knows the romance to be doomed.

The same emotional intensity is found in *A World of Love*, also with an Irish setting, written over twenty-five years later. Jane is the *ingénue* about to cross the threshold into the adult world of love. She is at Montfort, where her parents live, for the summer, in the company of her overbearing older cousin, Antonia. Jane finds a package of love-letters in the attic from Guy, who is now dead but was once the owner of Montfort and loved by both Jane's mother and Antonia; she precipitates a situation where the middle-aged characters in the book must confront the past. Guy begins to haunt Jane and the two older women. The novel is concerned with the pain and power of memory. The central scene is a dinner party at the refurbished castle of a *nouveau-riche* neighbour, where Jane takes her step over the threshold literally and emotionally, and the ghost of Guy appears in the empty chair at the table. As she enters the room the collection of men appears as a black and white mass, 'one abstract shirtfront'. It is not until the next day that we hear what they actually ate; for Jane the dinner party is totally concerned with her apprehension of Guy's presence, not unassisted by her first ever Martini. Food at Montfort is unattractive: beetroot, brawn, unset junket. When Jane's mother is delayed at the hairdresser's and is concerned about spoiling lunch, Jane counters with, 'Mother, you can't spoil rhubarb.' Jane's story is only beginning on the last page of the novel when she meets a man at Shannon Airport and 'they no sooner looked but they loved'.

At a luncheon party in the United States (Elizabeth Bowen lectured all over the States and was Lucy Martin Donnelly Fellow at Bryn Mawr College) a friend said that although he didn't believe in God, he did believe in ghosts. Elizabeth Bowen replied acerbically that she believed in God and ghosts; and the appearance of Guy in *A World of Love* is not an unusual event in her stories. Her wartime stories often have a haunted quality, stories like *Pink May*, *Green Holly*, and most frightening of all, *The Demon Lover*, the end of which terrified the young Iris Murdoch. In the short story *Foothold*, the ghost Clara disrupts a contented marriage as she takes over Janet's personality. The story opens with a welcoming breakfast for Thomas, the couple's weekend guest:

> '*Morning!' exclaimed Gerard, standing before the sideboard, napkin under his arm. 'Sleep well? There are kidneys here, haddock, if you prefer it, ham and boiled eggs —*'

But already Clara the ghost intrudes. Although at this stage the phantom presence is considered as something of a joke, Thomas realises that there is tension present and changes the subject:

— *'Forgive my being so purely carnal,' exclaimed Thomas suddenly, 'but this is the most excellent marmalade. Not gelatinous, not slimy. I never get quite the right kind. Does your cook make it?'*

By the time they are eating muffins at evening tea, Thomas has seen Clara himself and is beginning to realise how serious the situation is.

Breakfasts are always substantial in Elizabeth Bowen's stories. Her first published story, entitled *Breakfast*, opens confidently: ' "Behold, I die daily," thought Mr Rossiter, entering the breakfastroom.' The setting is a rather unpleasant boarding house and the personalities of Mr Rossiter's fellow guests are exposed by their breakfast eating habits. The effect is claustrophobic. Mr Rossiter pays Mrs Russell twenty-four shillings a week for the privilege of a 'comfortable sit-down' breakfast, which is in reality an unpleasant experience of clashing personalities and mottled bacon.

In *The Visitor*, a little boy comes down to breakfast in a strange house belonging to friends of his dying mother. To him the table resembles a battlefield:

On the table, the hosts of breakfast were marshalled into two opposing forces...the toast, eggs, bacon and marmalade had declared for Miss Dora; but the tea-pot and its vassals, the cruet and the honeycomb — beautifully bleeding in a flowered dish — were for Miss Emery to a man.'

Bowen often covers a child's viewpoint in a story. In *To the North*, a rather boring child, Pauline, provides a stolid balance to the febrile atmosphere as Emmeline and her cad, Markie, hurtle to their destruction. She experiences food with happy appetite; 'she ate gooseberry tart with short pastry and Camembert with a delicious oozy inside; her skirt-belt began to tighten, a guarantee of repletion unknown at school.'

Emmeline and Markie have a pleasant dinner in Markie's flat, where the food is sent up on a lift by a whistling cook, an experience that enchants Emmeline, although the meal is a tense one, all unresolved passion. Markie is not amused by Emmeline's immoderate laughter and explains that the whistle is to warn him that dinner is on its way in the lift:

'But supposing your cook couldn't whistle?'
'I suppose we should have a bell!'
'But why don't you have a bell anyhow?'
'I suppose because our cook can whistle.'

The intensity of *A World of Love*, the 'annihilation point of sensation', is overpoweringly present in *To the North*, and the end is both surprising and inevitable.

Eva Trout was Elizabeth Bowen's last novel, and something of a stylistic departure for her. There is a marvellous lunch which Bowen set in a favourite restaurant — it is dark and costly, its intimacy making all the diners seem like lovers. Constantine and Iseult are there to discuss the impossible Eva Trout. Food and wine are important to Constantine, but Iseult chooses *ris de veau* without properly consulting the menu and Constantine winces. He orders oysters for both of them:

Advancing upon their table came hosts of oysters. Salivating, he had to compress his lips: he leaned back, dotingly watching the feast set down.

For Iseult, greed had another dimension:

The very first she swallowed wrought a change in her. Greed softened and in a peculiar way spiritualised her abstruse beauty, with its touch of the schoolroom. Eating became her — more than once she had been fallen in love with over a meal.

Elizabeth Bowen is famous for her wartime stories. She said the war was the most exciting time of her life, and she remained in London as an air-raid warden. In 1941 she met Charles Ritchie, the Canadian diplomat, with whom she fell in love and who was with her when she died over thirty years later. Her wartime novel, *The Heat of the Day*, an unforgettable story of love and betrayal, is dedicated to him. Stella's lover Robert, whom she believes to be a Dunkirk hero, is really a traitor. She visits his ghastly home and meets his equally dreadful mother. One can imagine why he betrayed his country, if it meant change in the world of his upbringing; Robert tries to cut a cake at tea:

'You wouldn't think it was time we bought a new cake?'
'But that one has not been eaten,' objected Ernestine. 'I'm sure Mrs Rodney will take us as she finds us.'
'Happily for Mrs Rodney, she does not eat cake.'

Stella meets Harrison, a mystery man seemingly in the Secret Service and on the trail of Robert. He takes her out to dinner, a meal of cloying food and an increasing sense of horror as Stella realises that the price of Robert's safety is herself. The food reflects her emotional condition — lobster mayonnaise 'on a bed of greenstuff knifed into gripping ribbons'. It is the most frightening meal in all of Bowen's writing, as Stella struggles in Harrison's net, unable to come to terms with his power over her:

> *The considerable remains of the lobster were taken away; crumbs of coral, dribbles of greenery,...two double portions of fruit flan appeared.*

For Stella and Robert the situation is without hope. They have dinner together in a restaurant where they are known. Dining late, the atmosphere is soothing, a sensation of intimacy familiar to lovers of restaurants and lovers in restaurants.

> *Themselves in the friendly restaurant, they sat down; by this hour the place was emptying...the restaurant was waning, indifferently relaxing its illusion: for the late-comers a private illusion took its place. Their table seemed to stand on their own carpet; they had a sensation of custom, sedateness, of being inside small walls, as though dining at home again after her journey.*

PHEASANT SOUP

> Dinah added a tinful of ready-made pheasant soup and later sherry, to the liquid from the bones. The omelette, as sometimes does happen with those made under unfavourable conditions, turned out to be one of her best. Claret was enjoyed.
>
> *The Little Girls*

Veronica's daughter Rebecca tasted pheasant for the first time last winter and loved it. When she was little, someone said that she was six years old, going on thirty-two! That was when she used to 'help' Fionn in the kitchen, making bread and apple pies and strange, private things that looked like dog biscuits. The dog thought they were too. This recipe is for her, in the hope that a lifetime of new and exciting tastes awaits her.

> 2 pheasant carcasses
> 2 medium onions
> 2 carrots
> sage, thyme and parsley
> 2½ pt (1¼l) chicken stock
> ½ wine glass sherry
> juice of 1 lemon
> salt and pepper
> croûtons

Simmer the pheasant with the vegetables, herbs and stock until the meat falls off the bones. Pour the liquid through a sieve into a clean pot. Remove the bones and herbs from the residue, then liquidise the remainder and add to the strained liquid. Before serving, add the sherry and lemon juice, and season if necessary. Add the croûtons.
Serves four.

FILLET OF SOLE BAILE ÁTHA CLIATH

'Here come the fish: sole, they say — D'you know I thought for a moment...'
'What?' said Cecilia who could not help smiling.
'I thought for a moment we'd met.'

To the North

Elizabeth Bowen wrote a book on the Shelbourne Hotel at the instigation of her friend Cyril Connolly. It is really a sort of social history of Dublin, and one of the menus she describes for the Christmas of 1922 (a month after the last of the British troops had left the Free State) is decorated with shamrocks and written in a sort of Gaelic lettering, but in French. The plum pudding becomes *Pouding de Noël,* served with *Sauce au Cognac,* but mince pies retain their English name, defying any French interference. This is our version of the fish course.

2oz (60g) butter
4oz (120g) mushrooms, sliced
2oz (60g) flour
1 pt (600ml) milk
2 tsp mustard
salt and pepper
4oz (120g) grated cheddar
8 fillets of sole
8 potatoes, mashed
handful of chopped parsley
1 orange and 1 lemon, sliced

Melt the butter in a saucepan and cook the mushrooms until softened. Stir in the flour and then add one third of the milk, stirring all the time to avoid lumps. Add the rest of the milk. Continue to stir, and add mustard, salt and pepper, and lastly the grated cheese. Stir until smooth.

Poach the fillets of sole in a saucepan of simmering salted water for 5 minutes. Put the mashed potato around the edge of a gratin dish. Place the fish in the centre and pour the sauce onto the fish. Sprinkle with chopped parsley and garnish the dish around the sides with butterflies of orange and lemon slices.
Serves four.

WILD DUCK SALMI

Jane seemed to go off the air. She at last said: 'Hash.
Hash at that castle? No, it must have been salmi.'

A World of Love

Salmi is an eighteenth-century French word for ragoût of roasted game, stewed with wine or port. It is a perfect way to use up any sort of leftover game, and the aroma when the port is tipped into the pan is magic!

1 wild duck, cooked
1½ pt (900ml) chicken stock
1½oz (45g) butter
1 onion, sliced
6 mushrooms, sliced
1 tomato, chopped
1oz (30g) flour
1 wine glass port
1 tsp Marmite
salt and pepper
8 black olives, stoned and halved
handful of chopped parsley
8 potatoes, cooked and mashed

Pre-heat oven to 190°C (375°F, Gas mark 5).

To cook the duck, put it in a small ovenproof dish with ½ pt (300 ml) of chicken stock. Cover the bird with tinfoil and cook for three-quarters of an hour at 190°C, 375°F, Gas mark 5. Strip the meat from the duck, cut into slices and set aside. Melt the butter in a saucepan, add the vegetables and cook gently until softened. Stir in the flour. Cook for a minute and add the port, Marmite and the rest of the stock. Season with salt and pepper. Simmer for 10 to 15 minutes, then pour over the duck meat. Garnish with olives and parsley, and serve with mashed potatoes. Serves two.

ORANGE SOUFFLÉ

Anna, plunging the spoon and fork into the soufflé with that
frank greed one shows in one's own house when there is enough
of everything, said: 'Besides I thought you said that it was
instinctive.'

Death of the Heart

This recipe comes from the Scottish end of Veronica's family; her cousins Hector
and Sydney always served the most marvellous food and this soufflé has infiltrated
the collective cuisine of the entire family.

2½ tsp powdered gelatine
¼ cup hot water
4 eggs, separated
grated peel of the oranges
juice of 2 oranges
2oz (60g) castor sugar
½ pt (300ml) cream

Dissolve the gelatine in a teacup set in a bowl of hot water. In a large bowl stir the
egg yolks into the gelatine. Add the grated orange peel, juice and sugar. Whip the
egg whites and fold in. Whip the cream, fold in and leave to set.
Serves six.

SINK-THE-BISMARCK CHOCOLATE CAKE

This chocolate cake is a speciality of Danielstown's. I do believe it's a charm that they make it by, not a recipe.

The Last September

Reminiscing recently we both recalled a long-ago birthday party of Mary Kate's (Fionn's daughter) at which simply everything was made of chocolate. The table looked stunning and very decadent. A crowd of noisy little girls consumed everything and all went home with brown faces and ruined party frocks. Wonder how many were sick? Mary Kate recommends this cake for breakfast, but for that you'd need an iron constitution. Mind you, the battleship Bismarck had an iron constitution and look what happened to it!

> 6oz (180g) dark chocolate
> 6oz (180g) butter
> 6oz (180g) castor sugar
> 4 eggs, separated
> 3oz (90g) ground almonds
> 3oz (90g) flour

Preheat oven to 175°C (350°F, Gas mark 4).

Melt the chocolate in a bowl placed over a pot of boiling water. Beat the butter and sugar together with the egg yolks. Add the chocolate, almonds and flour. Whisk the egg whites until stiff, then fold in carefully. Pour the mixture into two greased 8in (20 cm) tins. Bake for 25 minutes. Cool and then fill and ice.

Icing

1 100g Mars bar
2 100g bars Bourneville chocolate
2 tbsp cream

Melt together in a bowl standing in a pot of boiling water. Add more cream if the mixture seems too stiff. Sandwich the two cakes together, then ice all over. Makes one cake.

GINGERBREAD

Mothers unpacked scones and potted-meat sandwiches or cut up gingerbread tensely but steadily, as though nothing were happening — or rather not happening.

The Little Girls

Gingerbread was rather a treat in Veronica's home in Manchester, as her mother's version had a rather toffeeish consistency, and once or twice had to be prised into slices with a chisel. This unlikely activity of her mother's greatly enhanced the flavour, and they used to insist that she overdid the treacle ever after. Veronica's youngest child is Stephen James who, while not being toffee-nosed, has yet a nose for toffee or any sweet thing. When very small he loved gingerbread men, so this recipe is specially for him.

> 8oz (240g) plain flour
> 1 tsp salt
> 1 tsp ground ginger
> 1 tsp baking powder
> 4oz (120g) butter
> 5oz (150g) brown sugar
> 4 eggs, separated
> 4 tbsp molasses *or*
>   2¹/₂ tbsp treacle
> 5oz (150g) natural yoghurt

Preheat oven to 175°C (350°F, Gas mark 4).

Sift the flour, salt, ginger and baking powder together. In another bowl, cream the butter until soft. Add the sugar and beat until smooth, then add the beaten egg yolks. In another bowl combine the molasses and yoghurt and, alternating with the flour mixture, add to the butter. Finally, fold in the stiffly beaten egg whites. Pour into a greased 1lb loaf tin.

Bake at 175°C (350°F, Gas mark 4) for 50 to 60 minutes, until a knife inserted in the middle comes out clean.

Remove from the oven and leave to stand in the tin for 10 minutes. Then slide a knife around the inside of the tin to loosen the gingerbread. Turn upside down and tap sharply on top of the tin. The gingerbread should come out cleanly.
Makes one loaf.

9

Patrick Kavanagh

Patrick Kavanagh, poet, was born on a small farm in Iniskeen, County Monaghan. His first book of poems *Ploughman and Other Poems* was published in 1938, as was an autobiographical novel *The Green Fool.* In 1939 he went to Dublin where he worked as a literary journalist. *The Great Hunger* (1942), a long and bitter poem about his Irish rural life, established him as an important poet. He and his brother Peter produced sixteen issues of *Kavanaghs' Weekly,* a satirical journal of literature and politics. Severe illness in 1955 prompted a spiritual renewal which confirmed his belief in God, infusing his poetry with new life. *Come Dance with Kitty Slobling* appeared in 1960, and his reputation as a poet outside Ireland was recognised with the *Collected Poems* of 1964. He died in Dublin.

Patrick Kavanagh   1904 to 1967

On many occasions I literally starved in Dublin. I often borrowed 'a shilling for the gas' when in fact I wanted the coin to buy a chop.

Note to the *Collected Poems*

Poverty and poetry were the cornerstones of Patrick Kavanagh's life. For him 'the big tragedy for the poet is poverty', and scratching an existence in Dublin could be as cruel and unrelenting as in the stony Monaghan he had left behind. Life in Monaghan had one definite advantage — a caring, bossy, efficient mother who made sure he was fed properly; in Dublin he had to fend for himself. He lived in Ballsbridge, a leafy civilised area of Dublin that he patrolled assiduously every day. Pembroke Road was his personal 'jungle'; and Raglan Road had a romantic association with a dark-haired beauty. He knew everyone on the streets, in the shops, in the bookies, in the pubs. On his diurnal promenade he stopped as many people as possible in order to talk to them, whether they wished it or not. He assumed a special identity, that of a Dublin character; he was a massive man with a large head, hatted, big farmer's hands, horn-rimmed glasses, usually carrying a newspaper and usually talking to himself, which rather frightened the local children. Fionn O'Reilly was one of them. The bath in the Pembroke Road flat bore witness to his culinary abilities: it was full to overflowing with empty sardine tins and old tea leaves; the tin-opener was the indispensable utensil. That wonderful poem, 'Advent', which begins,

We have tested and tasted too much, lover —
Through a chink too wide there comes in no wonder.
But here in the Advent-darkened room
Where the dry black bread and sugarless tea
Of penance claim back the luxury
Of a child's soul...

evokes the comfortless flat where black tea and dry bread was all there was on offer. Anthony Cronin remembers Kavanagh with affection in his book *Dead as Door Nails*. He rescues him one Christmas, treating the poet to steak and onions and whiskey instead of the old cold herring that Kavanagh said awaited him in the Ballsbridge flat. The first time Cronin invited him there, he asked him if he did his own cooking, and the reply was 'I sometimes boil an egg in the teapot, if you call that cooking'!

John Ryan was a good friend to Paddy Kavanagh and when he was editor of *Envoy* he often fed him at the Monument Café on Grafton Street. Kavanagh told him that one day he was walking by the Grand Canal when he found a mallard caught on the spikes of the railings. He extricated the duck and gave sincere assurances to his audience of worried little old ladies that he would take it immediately to the Cats and Dogs Home. He doubled back to his Pembroke Road flat where he roasted and consumed the poor bird. Perhaps his culinary skills were more developed than he liked to admit, for the duck was delicious: 'It melted in me mouth like butter.'

A favourite eating place was the Country Shop on St Stephen's Green, run by the Irish Countrywomen's Association. It is no longer there, alas, for it was a truly strange restaurant of different bars serving different food in different rooms, all with their own queues at lunchtime. One entered at the basement level, where the 'proper' three course lunch was served by waitresses, and was immediately assailed by the characteristic smell, not unpleasant, of cake and cabbage and turf. Perhaps it was a smell redolent of home for Kavanagh. It was popular with both very old ladies in tweeds and impecunious young students, and the afternoon teas were unsurpassable. Kavanagh's comment on this unique establishment was not exactly vintage Egon Ronay: 'You got your bellyful there and it was dainty.'

When Kavanagh first came to Dublin in 1939 it was with great expectations, for what better city could there be for a poet than one so rich in famous writers. AE (George Russell, the poet), always kind and encouraging towards new poetic talent, took him under his wing, and, as Kavanagh appeared to him to be the peasant-poet of Irish tradition, he was accepted by the establishment. The idyll did not last. Kavanagh might have looked like a badly-dressed, raw-boned, clumsy bogman (things mysteriously 'broke' in his proximity), but that exterior merely hid a highly developed and sophisticated intellect. Kavanagh abhorred cant and hypocrisy; his philosophy went beyond criticism and out of the reach of all the smug self-importance and humbug that he discovered in Dublin's literary crowd. His attacks were passionately voiced in vicious satire. The victims of his invective objected to his behaviour and Kavanagh became something of an outcast, vilified and slurred. Oliver St John Gogarty, in an ill-starred venture, took the publishers of *The Green Fool* to court for a sentence which suggested that his parlour-maid might be his mistress.

Seamus O'Sullivan, while watching a man pushing a cart of manure up the road, commented, 'I see Paddy Kavanagh's moving'. After the publication of *The Great Hunger* in 1942, the local hacks gave the poet a title that one simply shouldn't reproduce in a cookery book. When *The Great Hunger* was banned, Kavanagh commented that it was probably a good idea to do so because if a policeman could understand it, it probably was not a very good poem anyway!

Kavanagh wrote:

> *As I have remarked on many an occasion*
> *Living in the country is a hard old station.*

and yet it is the country that provides the backdrop to much of his work, both poetry and, as he has it, 'pruse'. Tarry Flynn, a farmer, who is also a visionary and dreamer, works on the family farm:

> *All day he sprayed the potatoes, and nothing was happening except his being.*
> *Being was enough, it was the worship of God.*

Tarry is enthralled by the beauty of the natural world; to him the daisies are thrilling and the clay wondrous. He loves all common things, stones and grass, nettles and sunlight, potatoes, and the wild flowers he cannot name. In a narrow, Catholic, repressed society he is considered an idiot, and even his mother who loves him cannot understand his interest in books. Mrs Flynn feeds the family well on a filling, if unvarying, diet based on their own produce — pigs and potatoes, chickens and turnips. The potatoes are washed for dinner in the tubs outside the front door, and boiled in their skins. The cooking is performed over an open fire; the water has to be carried from the well:

> *Aggie had gone to the well for water. When she came in she offered to keep an eye on the pot and not let it boil all over the floor. She had also to see that the delicate chicken who was rolled up in a black stocking in a porringer by the hob did not get scalded or burned.*

Now there's a delicacy to conjure with — chicken in a black stocking, or *poussin au bas noir*, try looking that one up in *Larousse Gastronomique*. But while Tarry might dream of unattainable virgins, the animals at least have a normal life, and Tarry eats a raw egg he finds in the manger: 'It was not that he liked raw eggs but he believed that raw eggs produced great virility.

Stallions got a dozen raw eggs in a bucket of new milk every day during the season.' And when Tarry's mother offers him the last egg (before asking his three sisters; unmarried girls are only 'pratie-washers') he refuses it for 'Sure, two's any God's amount'.

In *The Green Fool* Kavanagh remembers an Easter picnic when he was a child. The children had no money to buy the food so they decided to collect empty bottles and return them to the shop in Inniskeen for the 'empties' money. Kavanagh and his friend laboriously collect four and a half dozen bottles, only to be offered threepence a dozen by the mean shopkeeper. But somehow or other the longed-for picnic happens:

We had our feast after all with jam and syrup, three kinds of currant bread and three kinds of eggs. Mrs Gorman supplied the eggs, goose egg, hen eggs, and green duck eggs. We held our feast on the top of Gorman's hill under an old white thorn. We made our fire and boiled our kettle over it, we hung the kettle by a wire from a sour-looking limb of the white thorn. There were seven of us at the feast, including the two dogs.

Dare one add 'Ate in Arcadia Eggo'?

Pig slaughtering is a festive affair, something to be celebrated:

One by one the pigs were dragged out by a steel gaff and killed right beside our front door. Nobody felt sick or squeamish...It was a memorable morning; the blood of dawn was being poured over the hills, and of that other blood we only thought how much black pudding it would make.

The occasion is marked by a feast of a breakfast: 'Tea, bread and two eggs for every man, woman and child; it was a gala day.'

Kavanagh loved the threshing, when farmers would swop labour to get the job done in the shortest time. There were always lots of girls in the kitchens:

Around to all the threshings came the marriageable girls of the district — to cook. At one threshing I counted seven cooks in the kitchen. They appeared very busy when I called at the door. Seeing that it was only myself was there they slowed down a bit. Twelve mugs of buttermilk stood on the table. The large pot of potatoes was boiling over the fire, and beside it simmered another pot of cabbage already boiled.

'Have yez much help?' One of the girls asked.

140

'Fair,' I said.
'Will yez be done before tay-time?' the woman of the house asked.
'We may,' I replied.
'That would be great,' her daughter said, 'we won't have the trouble of making tay if we keep back the dinner.'

The little things of life were his inspiration — 'potatoes and old boots', and life itself a cause for loving celebration:

This is what love does to things: the Rialto Bridge,
The main gate that was bent by a heavy lorry,
The seat at the back of a shed that was a suntrap,
Naming these things is the love-act and its pledge;
For we must record love's mystery without claptrap,
Snatch out of time the passionate transitory.

THE IRISH FRY

I wasn't listening to AE. I was worried over the poor impression I was making. I was hungry — For poetry? Yes, but I was also physically hungry, and an empty stomach is a great egoist, and a bad listener to anything save the fizz of rashers on a pan.

The Green Fool

In Ireland on a Saturday evening the traditional meal was always the big fry: a mouth-watering mélange of sausages, black and white pudding, rashers and eggs, with the addition, if desired, of tomatoes, mushrooms and fried bread. It is still a popular meal but do not bring the cholesterol counter to the table!

The fry is also considered the proper Irish breakfast, but if you're a member of the militant muesli brigade, such a meal is an occasion of sin. If you're on holiday in Ireland and staying in a hotel or guesthouse, it's a treat of a way to start the day.

rashers of bacon
sausages
black pudding
white pudding
tomatoes
mushrooms
eggs
fried bread
potato cakes
lamb cutlets
lamb sweetbreads
lamb kidneys

Rashers can be grilled or fried. Fried is best if you are making fried bread or potato cakes. Sausages are best grilled because of their high fat content. Black and white pudding is already cooked and should be peeled and sliced, then fried or grilled to heat it thoroughly and to crisp the outside. The tomatoes, mushrooms and egg are nicest fried in the bacon fat. The fried bread and potato cakes are done last to use up the fat. Cutlets, sweetbreads and kidneys are sometimes added at teatime. Wash the sweetbreads and kidneys in cold water to get the blood off. Cut in half, remove the core and the membrane. They can be grilled or fried, but watch them carefully, as they cook quite quickly (5-10 minutes). Cutlets are best grilled, unless you are very keen on mutton fat.

CHAMP

George told me. 'Me grand-uncle was in Monaghan gaol for a debt of eleven shillings. Me granny brought him his dinner of champ every day. Twenty one and a half Irish miles to Monaghan, she'd have the champ warm enough to melt the butter.'

The Green Fool

Champ is a rare dish nowadays — a combination of mashed potato and leeks or onions. It is a cousin to the other known delicacy — thump. When Veronica's son Jason was a patrol-leader in Dalkey Sea Scouts, this dish was considered easy and filling — the main priorities in camp cooking. Thump, a death-defying mash of potatoes, carrots, processed peas and tinned corn beef, gets its name from the extraordinary noise it makes as it hits the tin plate. We don't recommend you make it unless you own to masochistic tendencies; we do however recommend you make the champ, which is good with steak or chops, or with that ubiquitous Irish main course, the boiled bacon.

8 medium potatoes
6 scallions (spring onions) or 3 leeks
4oz (120g) butter
salt and pepper
parsley

Peel and halve the potatoes. Chop the onions or leeks. Boil together until soft (about 30 minutes). Drain the vegetables and mash with 2oz (60g) of the butter, adding salt and pepper to taste. Just before serving, make a hole in the top of the mound of mashed potato and add the remaining butter. Sprinkle with chopped parsley.
Serves four.

PORCINE PLEASURES

You perfumed my clothes with weasel itch
You fed me on swinish food.

Stony Grey Soil

A friend of ours, Chris, has a way with pork; no, not just a way, a true talent. No coward she, she once bought a pig, installed it in the garden while it was being fattened, and was present at its demise. This is called being thorough. The flesh was transformed into an impressive array of sausages, ham, pickled pork, salamis, pâtés, black puddings made with cream and brandy, rillettes and bacon for rashers. Few houses anywhere could boast the sight that met you on opening a bedroom door — an entire guestroom hung with sausages and salamis at varying stages of maturity; the general effect was that of rather bizarre Christmas decorations designed by a manic pork butcher.

HEAD CHEESE

Head cheese, admittedly, is an unusual concoction which resembles a rough country pâté. But trust us, it makes a wonderful starter or lunch dish accompanied by a good salad and fresh bread.

1 pig's head
2 trotters
2 pig's tails
2 bay leaves

Place all the above in a large pot, cover with water, put the lid on, bring to the boil and simmer for 5 hours. When cool, remove the meat from the bones. Discard the fat and skin; brains may be included, also the tongue. Chop the meat into small pieces. Add a little fat to taste, preferably from the trotters as this is more gelatinous.

4 shallots
1 small carrot
1 bunch parsley
1$\frac{1}{2}$ tsp pepper or allspice
$\frac{1}{4}$ tsp cinnamon
$\frac{1}{4}$ tsp ground clove
$\frac{1}{4}$ tsp nutmeg

Chop the vegetables and parsley finely, add the spices and mix well; add to the meat mixture. If it is too dry, add some of the stock. The mixture should be moist but not sloppy. This amount will fill two $\frac{1}{2}$lb loaf tins and should, if possible, be pressed, as it gives a better consistency and is easier to slice. Leave overnight in the fridge. The 'cheese' will keep for several days if refrigerated. This is the cheapest dish to make in our book.

FRIED HERRING AND MACKEREL

I went home to my room and fried herrings on the gas-ring.
The landlord, when he came home, caught the smell of fried fish.
He was furious and half-drunk. Normally he appeared a very
polite fellow, but now he swore.
'Leave this room when your week is up,' he said.
'Okay,' I said.
Fish, and herrings in particular, are supposed to be good for the
brain...

The Green Fool

Kavanagh used to say he only had a bit of cold herring at home if a friend suggested treating him to a meal. We assume you are in possession of more than one gas-ring so that you can make the sauce to accompany the fried herring. The fish must be as fresh as possible to taste the way it should. Mackerel may be substituted for herring. Both are inexpensive fish and must be eaten the day you buy them.

    4 whole fresh herring or mackerel
    lemon juice
    salt and pepper
    1 egg, beaten
    oatflakes
    2 tbsp sunflower oil
    1 tbsp butter or margarine

To prepare the fish, remove the scales with the back of a knife, cut off the head and remove the guts. Wash, dry, then fold the fish out flat and remove as many of the bones as you can without too much damage to the flesh. Sprinkle the insides with lemon juice and season. Dip the fish first into the beaten egg, then into the oatflakes, and fry in the oil with the butter or margarine. Serve with mashed potato, and tomato and mushroom sauce.

Tomato and Mushroom Sauce

    1 large onion
    1 clove garlic
    1 tin chopped tomatoes
    4oz (120g) mushrooms, sliced

Peel and chop the onion and garlic. Fry in a little oil until soft. Add the tomatoes and mushrooms. Simmer for 10 to 15 minutes until the mushrooms are cooked. Serves four.

CHERRY CAKE

The Matron once inquired if I was feeling hungry. I was and hunger was no name for it. I was now five weeks without a bit of solid food. Every night, I dreamt of lovely currant and cherry cakes.

The Green Fool

Kavanagh, who was in hospital with typhoid fever, might not dream of the sort of cherry cakes that are available today — rather nasty, dry Madeira cakes with candied cherries dotted through them. The cherry cake, if one uses any of the pre-World War II recipes before the rationing of eggs and dried fruit had such a catastrophic effect on baking generally, should be a light, moist but eggy mixed fruit cake, with the emphasis on cherries. Buy the best ones you can get. It is particularly good for lunch boxes, being a splendid, everyday 'cutting cake'.

12oz (360g) butter
1lb (480g) castor sugar
8 whole eggs beaten
1½lb (720g) plain flour
1lb (480g) raisins
8oz (240g) candied peel
1lb (480g) candied cherries
rind 2 oranges
8oz (240g) ground almonds
¼ pt (150ml) brandy
1 tsp salt
½oz (15g) mixed spice
Two 8in (20cm) cake tins

Preheat oven to 160°C (325°F, Gas mark 3).

Beat the butter with the sugar; add a tablespoon each of the eggs and the flour alternately, beating well all the time. Then add the fruit, orange rind and the ground almonds. Mix well, add the brandy, salt and spices and beat again.

Grease and line the tins with greaseproof paper. Divide the mixture between the 2 tins. Bake for 2 to 2½ hours. Test with a skewer. If it comes out clean, the cakes are done. If you do not have teenage children, you can safely halve the amounts of the ingredients.
Makes one cake.

BLACKBERRY COBBLER

> During the War money grew on the tops of the bushes.
> Blackberries were five shilling a stone. Rocksavage farm was the
> home of briars, rich fruit-bearing briars ignored by all the money-
> grabbers. Very few people ate blackberries, the one man who did
> we thought a bit touched on that account. Myself and two sisters
> were sent out each morning with cans and porringers.
>
> *The Green Fool*

After reading Kavanagh's two novels one wonders if Irish country people ever ate any fruit at all, though Kavanagh admits a liking for the 'black, juicy fruit' when he was older, a liking he shared with his dog Sam.

Both of us have childhood memories of blackberry picking and have brought our own children out foraging in the hedgerows of counties Dublin and Wicklow. The scratches on the hands and legs and the indescribable stains on the T-shirts are forgotten in the enjoyment of jam and pies.

Our decision to include a recipe for Blackberry Cobbler was not because Patrick Kavanagh's father was a part-time mender of boots — that sort of cheap shot just isn't our line.

> 1lb (480g) cooking apples, peeled and sliced
> 4oz (120g) castor sugar
> 2 tbsp water
> 1lb (480g) blackberries
> 6oz (180g) self-raising flour
> 2oz (60g) butter
> ¼ pt (150ml) milk, approx
> 1 egg, beaten

Preheat oven to 200°C (400°F, Gas mark 6).

Stew the apple gently with half the sugar and about 2 tablespoons of water in a heavy saucepan for 10 to 15 minutes, until soft. Stir in the blackberries, and add more sugar if the blackberries are not all very ripe. Bring to the boil gently, then set aside. Sift the flour and rub in the butter or margarine. Add the rest of the sugar, then stir the milk in slowly until the mixture is a nice soft dough. Take care not to make it too wet. Turn out on a floured board, knead gently and roll out to ½in (1cm) thickness. Cut with a 6cm scone cutter. Brush the tops with beaten egg. Put the fruit mixture in an oven-proof dish. Arrange the circles of dough on top. Bake for 15 minutes.
Serves six.

10

Molly Keane

Molly Keane, novelist, was born in Wexford of the Anglo-Irish gentry. Hunting was her passion and her religion. To avoid social rejection by her 'set' she wrote her early plays and novels under the pseudonym M J Farrell. *Conversation Piece, Devoted Ladies, Full House* and *Rising Tide* were all great successes in the thirties. Her plays were West End hits and were always directed by Sir John Gielgud, a lifelong friend. Her creative gift was disrupted by the grief of her husband's death, but when her two daughters were married she began to write again. *Good Behaviour*, published in 1981, was short-listed for the Booker Prize. This was followed by *Time After Time* in 1983, and *Loving and Giving* in 1988. Her wicked black humour and talent for social satire have made her books best sellers all over the world. Mrs Keane lives in Ardmore, County Waterford.

Molly Keane   b. 1904

The list of possibilities is long, the pattern changeable. Any
trouble taken is well spent if it inspires an early interest in that
life-long adventure open to all: food and its cooking.
Molly Keane's Nursery Cooking

Molly Keane has a special talent for food. As she is a wonderful cook, it is
no surprise that she has written an excellent cookery book. Food to her is
one of the great pleasures of life, an abiding interest that she shared with
her husband and was pleased to pass on to her two daughters. Mrs Keane
had a hungry childhood. Trays of grim food were sent to the nursery from
the kitchen, skirmishes in the interminable warfare waged between Nanny
and Cook. Inedible, lumpy porridge, dark-veined rabbit legs and eggs only
on Sundays resulted in a thin, sickly child who, with her brother, went out
on foraging expeditions to supplement their meagre diet. Cook, presumably
to spite Nanny, would hand out an illicit scone, left-over rashers or a bit of
bread dipped in sugar. The garden, guarded by the vigilant head gardener
and a forbidding aunt who occasionally allowed them five minutes in the
raspberry patch, was the scene of their predations. They stole fruit and nuts
whenever they could and even took handfuls of the chopped carrots and
turnips meant for the cattle. That aunt also gave Molly Keane a guilt
complex about enjoying food, as desire for a second helping signified
seriously deviant behaviour; it was a complex that took years to demolish.

The food that was brought into the kitchen of the Big House must have
been wonderful: freshly picked fruit and vegetables in season, butter, eggs
and milk from the farm, and all that was provided by gun and rod.
Shooting and fishing formed an important part of the pattern of
Ascendancy life. When the servants rebel in *Good Behaviour* in their strike
for 'real' food, it is because 'the salmon has them killed', served to them
daily without respite. In spite of all this bounty the standard of cooking was
abysmal in the Irish country house. In all probability this was due to the
cluelessness of its mistress. Mrs Keane's own mother knew nothing of food
and its preparation; cooks were in bountiful supply, and if they couldn't
read their Mrs Marshall or Mrs Beeton, they could always be replaced. It
was all very uncivilised.

At least the appalling and inadequate diet made perfect copy for the childhood meals that are described in her novels. Nicandra in *Loving and Giving* is forced to sit over her uneaten spinach for hours, and Aroon St Charles in *Good Behaviour* calls the nursery food 'quite poisonously disgusting'. She lists the enormities of horrible porridge, sausages for birthdays only, rabbit stews and custards dotted with horrid holes.

The credit for initiating Molly Keane in the appreciation of good food lay with a dear friend who was simply an exception to the rule and who employed the services of a talented cook named Murphy. Holidays in her lovely old house in Tipperary opened the doors of gastronomic experience so that when Molly Keane travelled abroad she found herself fascinated by foreign food and the pleasure of ordering unfamiliar meals.

A reversal in circumstances led Mrs Keane to learn the art of cooking. She was very much a daughter of the Ascendancy, and her days were filled with the activities traditionally associated with this way of life. Paramount was hunting, so well described in *Red Letter Days* where the women performed in the field with legendary courage and nerveless dash. The world of hunting, shooting and fishing does not appear to have changed very much from that described so lovingly by Somerville and Ross in their RM stories. Like Somerville and Ross, Molly Keane shocked her mother by her determination to earn her living by her pen, and like them she was very successful.

But when her husband died at the early age of thirty-six, Mrs Keane was left with a Big House, little money and two very young daughters to bring up alone. At first she had help from Mary-Brigid, an inspired cook who depended on heavenly guidance. Later, there was a Swiss au-pair called Elspeth, whose cooking was of a rare perfection. To find out what Mrs Keane cooked, and Mary-Brigid and Elspeth too, one has only to read *Molly Keane's Nursery Cooking*, which is a pleasure to browse through and to use. The title is somewhat misleading, as its appeal is far wider than the nursery and its denizens. If the enthusiastic Keane fan wishes to know how to make 'Devilled Chicken's Legs to Eat with the Fingers' or 'Potatoes with Pennies', then this is the book to read, and who could resist Mary Brigid's Broken Glass Pudding?

Time after Time is patently a novel written by a person who not only understands but practises the art of good cooking. Jasper lives with his three sisters in a Big House in straitened circumstances and endless malice. He is in charge of the kitchen, which is exclusively his domain, one of sordid filth and rotting smells, inhabited by an evil cat called Mister Minkles and his many wives. Cooking is Jasper's passion — he is a creator of wonderful meals, and is himself an inspired creation, elegant and elderly, vicious and erratic. Mrs Keane once attended a special dinner in her honour in Paris. There was an animated discussion by the journalists and critics present on the character of Jasper. The guests could not imagine how such a gentle and delightful lady could be the begetter of the wicked Jasper. Mrs Keane listened quietly for some time until finally she jumped to her feet and with a 'Mais Jasper, c'est moi!', she stole the show.

Her gift for black comedy is apparent in Jasper's construction of a pigeon pie;

> *Beef? He shook his head to himself.*
> *Wait, wait a moment — where had he put them away those perfect leftovers for the dogs' dinners? Actually he had put them in the dogs' dinners. What went in could come out and go under the scullery tap, perhaps.*
> *...A purist in his cooking, he stood out against stock cubes. Black pepper, coriander, bayleaf, hard-boiled eggs...*

It is with evil relish that he informs his sisters of the beef's provenance, after they've eaten and enjoyed the pigeon pie, doing so with a 'nearly rat-like grin'!

Molly Keane has said that meals only occur in her books to advance the action; her consciousness of pace and progress seems very much that of the dramatist, and it is no surprise that *Time after Time* worked so well as a television film, for she sees her stories in strongly visual terms. The example that she likes herself is Aunt Tossie's dinner party in *Loving and Giving*. The preparation for the party, the party itself and the hunt ball that follows take up the whole of part two of the book. The sole, which is to be served in a 'miasma of herb-scented butter', has to come from a fish-monger far away, champagne is hunted from the cellars, and the bogs incessantly are shot for masses of snipe for Mrs Geary's famous snipe pudding. The crowning glory of the dinner is to be a really beautiful trifle.

Aunt Tossie becomes euphoric at the dinner party; high with social success and pleasure in her beloved niece Nicandra's beauty, she drinks far too much champagne. The image of her rooting around inside the snipe pudding as she searches for a dear little bird corpse in its delicious sauce reveals Molly Keane's writing at its comic best. The climax of the dinner party shows her at her most wicked, for when the inimitable trifle is displayed for the guests' pleasure — an enormous mountain of cream peaked with a single cherry — so is Aunt Tossie's large left breast which has worked loose of its black velvet moorings.

Good Behaviour, published in 1981, marked the revival of Molly Keane's writing career after an interval of twenty years. The opening scene is a shocker as we watch Aroon St Charles kill her mother with loving kindness over a spoonful of perfectly made rabbit quenelle. Aroon unfolds her own story of rejection and lost love as we realise that she has been the emotional dupe for both her parents and for her brother and his friend. Hubert and Richard adopt her as their mascot, the indispensable girl of the trio. To gain their attention and make them laugh she gives a breathtaking display of gluttony. At dinner before a ball, she eats nearly a whole side of smoked salmon (one of Molly Keane's favourite treats) with an entire lemon, most of a duck, four meringues, four pêches melbas, mushrooms and marrow on toast followed by cheese. In *Good Behaviour*, Mrs Keane gives the recipe for a White Lady, the cocktail that she and her set consumed in large quantities before parties and balls. A true blast from the twenties, this concoction of one third Cointreau, one third gin and one third lemon juice is guaranteed to put you in the mood.

Molly Keane is an ardent admirer of her literary precursors Somerville and Ross, and can quote liberally from the RM stories; her comic vision, if anything, is blacker and more malicious than theirs, and her books far more risqué than they could have ever imagined. Mrs Keane never knew Edith Somerville, but one cannot help thinking that the latter, belonging to the same tradition, would have enjoyed the company of this gentle, frail woman with the brightest of brains and an acute sense of the ridiculous. Mrs Keane's conversation is outrageous and witty, peppered with French phrases, twenties slang and the odd naughty word. Her charm is irresistible, as she wonders why the National University of Ireland conferred on her an honorary doctorate 'when I can't even spell', and then laughs as she puts the question: 'Dear children, did you know I'm awfully big in Bulgaria?'

HUNTING TEA

'...it's Teresa's night out so I brought ye a hunting tea — poor
Mrs Lennon's poached eggs and rashers.' The eggs were perfect,
swelling primly on large slices of buttered toast, the lightened dust
of cayenne blown over their well-matched pearls.

Good Behaviour

Hunting and the Anglo-Irish are inseparable. Brendan Behan's definition of the
class as 'a Protestant on a horse' is understandable if rather narrow. The women of
Molly Keane's time and that of Edith Somerville's, had the reputation of utter
recklessness; they rode without a nerve in their bodies. Fionn used to hunt, and she
assures everyone that the appetite one has after a day out with hounds is colossal. In
Red Letter Days, Mrs Keane, a great exponent of the sport of kings, tells us that the
best of all teas at the end of a perfect day was eggs and bacon and potato cakes,
preceded by whiskey.

Fry the potato cakes on a pre-heated frying pan with a generous amount of oil
until golden brown. Grill the rashers until crispy, then transfer both the rashers and
the potato cakes to the oven to keep hot. Poach the eggs, at least two per person,
and season with paprika for added heat!

See the Somerville and Ross recipe for potato cakes.

DAGMAR MURPHY'S WATERCRESS SOUP

'Tell me again about your watercress soup,' she might ask. And he
would almost tell her, then veer into eel soup — he knew the
nuns would be hard put to capture a conger.

Time after Time

Mrs Keane admits to a great liking for soups of all kinds and has some lovely
recipes in her own cookery book. This one belongs to Veronica's mother —
Veronica remembers watching her with fascination as a small child, as she
competently cooked the family lunch while seldom removing her eyes from the
book she was engrossed in at the time. Definitely the right woman for a literary
cookbook!

> 1oz (30g) butter
> 2 leeks, thinly sliced
> 1 small onion, chopped
> 8oz (240g) potato, diced
> 2 bunches of watercress
> 1 pt (600ml) chicken stock
> salt and pepper
> ½ pt (300ml) milk
> croûtons to garnish, if desired

Melt the butter in the pan, add the leeks and onions. Fry for 5 minutes without
browning. Add the potato and cook for 2 minutes. Meanwhile remove the stalk
from the watercress and roughly chop the leaves. Add to the pan with the stock.
Add salt and pepper to taste.

Bring to the boil. Cover the pan and simmer for 25 to 30 minutes. Blend until
smooth. Pour into a bowl and stir in the milk. Chill or serve hot.
Serves six.

SALMON KEDGEREE

'Shut up, you prurient old thing,' he said, shovelling in his kedgeree — salmon kedgeree, Nicandra noticed. There followed a silence that Nicandra could neither interrupt nor question — they were the Grown-Ups.

Loving and Giving

Kedgeree has the reputation of lurking on silver dishes on every sideboard in every Irish Big House novel, or British country house who-dun-it. A hangover from British Raj days, it was traditionally a breakfast dish. We have discovered it to be the most appetising way of using up salmon leftovers, and the creamy texture is good.

1lb (480g) salmon
parsley
thyme
a wedge of lemon
10oz (300g) rice
4 hardboiled eggs
1/4 pt (150ml) cream
1 1/2oz (45g) butter
salt and pepper

If you have no leftover salmon, poach 1lb (480g) salmon in a saucepan of lightly salted boiling water with the parsley, thyme and lemon for 20 minutes. Then skin, bone and flake. Cook the rice and hardboil the eggs (10 mins) at the same time. Cut the eggs in small pieces. Heat the cream and butter in a saucepan, with salt and pepper, until hot. Add the salmon, rice and eggs to the cream, combining the ingredients gently so as not to break up the egg and fish too much. Serve in a pile on a hot dish with some brown bread or hot buttered toast.
Serves six.

GAME PIE

Days in advance the bogs had been walked and snipe shot for that
famous snipe pudding of Mrs Geary's — a pudding more gently
extraordinary than any game pie.

Loving and Giving

Every Christmas, Fionn's husband makes huge amounts of high-walled game pies.
Christmas drinks are accompanied by delicious wedges of these pies served with
home-made chutney and a selection of mustards. The pies are lined with pork and
filled with chopped delicacies: venison, pigeon, pheasant, wild duck. They are not
the easiest things in the world to make but are so special and satisfying that the
effort is well worth while. Not so much 'gently extraordinary' as robustly satisfying.

Pastry

> 1lb (480g) strong white flour
> pinch of salt
> 4oz (120g) butter
> 1 egg

Sieve the flour and salt; rub in the butter, then add the egg and a little cold water to
mix to a paste. Put in the fridge to get cold, then roll it out to about ¼ inch
thickness and line a 10in (25cm) spring-form cake tin.

Mince

> 2lb (1kg) lean pork pieces
> ½lb (240g) lean bacon pieces
> ¼lb (120g) hard fat
> 2 tsp chopped sage
> ¼ tsp each of cinnamon, nutmeg and allspice
> pepper but *no salt*
> 1 dessertspoon anchovy essence

Preheat oven at 200°C (400°F, Gas mark 6).

Ask your butcher to mince the meat and fat for you, as it will save you a lot of time
and energy. Add the sage, spices and anchovy essence and mix well. Put a layer of
mince over the pastry on the sides and the bottom of the tin.

Game

Put the game in a heavy casserole with one glass of red wine. Cover and cook gently until half done. You will need about 3lb of game meat to fill this size tin. Hare and venison give a good strong flavour to the pie; pheasant, wild duck and pigeon breasts are excellent. If you only have a small amount of game, supplement it with chicken.

Fill the tin with game, then top it up with a layer of mince. Wet the edges of the pastry and place a lid of pastry on top. Press firmly at the edges to seal. Cut a hole in the centre and brush with beaten egg.

Put the cake tin in a roasting dish to catch the juices which will overflow. Bake at 200°C (400°F, Gas mark 6) for 20 minutes, then lower the heat to 150°C (300°F, Gas mark 2) for a further 2 hours.

Leave the pie to cool overnight, then pour the gelatine into the hole in the top. Be sure your pie is chilled or the gelatine will run out.

Gelatine

> 6 pig's trotters
> 1 bayleaf
> bouquet garni
> 1 onion and 1 carrot
> 5 pt (2½l) water

Place all the ingredients in a pot, bring to the boil and simmer for 6 hours. Cool, strain, and skim off the fat. Use at the point of setting. Alternatively, you can make a strong commercial gelatine using water which has been boiled with the herbs and vegetables and some of the stock from the game.
Serves eight to ten.

RABBIT QUENELLES WITH SORREL SAUCE

I lifted the silver lid off the hot plate to smell those quenelles in a
cream sauce. There was just a hint of bayleaf and black pepper,
not a breath of the rabbit foundation. Anyhow, what could be
more delicious and delicate than a baby rabbit?

Good Behaviour

Mrs Keane thought it fairly hilarious when we described our Herculean efforts in
forcing a rabbit, admittedly dead and boned but raw, through a sieve when we were
following Mrs Marshall's instructions to the letter. (Mrs Marshall ran a cookery
school in the 1880s, and wrote marvellous cookery books and had the last word on
how to perform culinary feats such as passing dead rabbits through a sieve.) The
scene resembled those awful pictures in the *National Geographic* of natives cooking
floppy monkeys. Preparing dishes like quenelles is considerably easier nowadays,
with the electric blender to do the hard work. Still, it is easier if the rabbit is cooked
first, or chicken or eel or....

> 1lb (480g) rabbit meat
> 1oz (30g) butter
> 2oz (60g) flour
> ¼ pt (150ml) chicken stock
> 2 eggs
> 1 tbsp cream
> salt and pepper

Stock Ingredients

> 1 large onion, chopped
> bouquet garni
> 1 large carrot, chopped
> salt and pepper
> ½ pt (300ml) dry white wine
> water to cover

Cook the rabbit in the stock ingredients by simmering gently for 45 minutes.
Reserve the stock for the sauce. Remove the meat from the bones and mince it
finely.

Make panada by melting butter, adding in the flour and cooking slightly. Add
stock and stir vigorously until a paste is formed (like in choux pastry). Cool panada

and add to meat. Pound together with a wooden spoon, add seasoning, eggs and cream. Pass the mixture through a sieve.

Form quenelles with 2 dessertspoons dipped in hot water. Poach gently in water which is not quite boiling for 15 minutes.

Sorrel Sauce

> 8oz (240g) sorrel
> ³/₄oz (20g) unsalted butter
> 2 tbsp flour
> Approx 1¹/₂ pt (900ml) rabbit stock
> ¹/₄ pt (150ml) cream
> 2oz (60g) unsalted butter, cut into small cubes

Parboil the sorrel for a few seconds, drain, stew gently in butter for 15 to 20 minutes, then purée.

Melt the butter in a saucepan. Add the flour and cook gently, while stirring, for about a minute, without letting it colour. Add the stock slowly while continuing to stir, then cook with the saucepan pulled to the side of the heat until the roux is thickened and smooth.

Whisk the sorrel purée into the sauce, adding as much cream as it can support without becoming too thin, then return it to the heat. Whisk in the cubed butter and pour over the quenelles.

Serves four.

PIGEON PIE

> When his hands were warm and limber, Jasper resumed the
> preparation of the pigeon pie. His mind floated forward in
> inspired construction...there were a few mushrooms somewhere
> in a paper bag, and he remembered rashers of streaky bacon,
> stiffening in age, too salty for breakfast, perfect for pie.
>
> *Time after Time*

Years ago, when Fionn's son Aillil was only six, we were on holiday in France and
ordering lunch in rather an elegant restaurant. We were wondering what the
children would like but were probably far more interested in our own orders when
Aillil's little voice shouted, 'Pigeons, please'. It was the start of a happy relationship
with super food, for he ate every bit. Mind you, he puts honey on his sausages — a
bit bizarre.

> 1lb (480g) rump steak
> 4 eggs
> 4 pigeon breasts
> ¼ pt (150ml) gravy
> ½ tsp salt
> 1 tsp pepper

Preheat oven to 160°C (325°F, Gas mark 3).

Cut the steak into 6 pieces. Boil the eggs for 10 minutes and remove shells. Lay the
steak in the bottom of a pie dish and the pigeons on top. Halve the eggs and place
them around the pigeons; season, then add the gravy. Grease the edge of the dish
and line it with a strip of pastry. Moisten with cold water and cover the pie with
pastry, pressing the edges firmly. Make a hole in the centre and bake at 160°C for 2
hours.

Pastry

> 9oz (270g) flour
> 2 tbsp cold water
> juice of half a lemon
> ½lb (240g) butter

Moisten the flour with the water and lemon juice, knead flat; put the butter in the centre, and fold over. Roll out four times and repeat; dredge flour over each time as necessary. Leave it in the fridge to get cold, then use.

Serves four.

11

Samuel Beckett

Samuel Beckett, poet, playwright and dissector of contemporary angst, found family constraints and academic life at Trinity College Dublin suffocating. He left Ireland for a restless sojourn in Europe, before settling in Paris where he found the personal freedom he sought. He was one of James Joyce's assistants on *Finnegans Wake* until a romantic misunderstanding with Joyce's daughter Lucia disrupted his relationship with the master. His courage as a member of the French Resistance earned him the Croix de Guerre in 1945. Literary fame, however, did not arrive until 1953 when *Waiting for Godot* was received with acclaim. The subsequent plays and novels displayed an increasingly stark vision of the human condition, populated by backs to the wall characters holding onto existence by their fingernails. Characters like Winnie, who is buried up to her waist in the play *Happy Days*, or Nagg and Nell in their dustbins in *Endgame*, created new and exciting images in contemporary drama. His humour was mortally black but always compelling. He was awarded the Nobel Prize for literature in 1969. Beckett died in Paris.

Samuel Beckett   1906 to 1989

Murphy's fourpenny lunch was a ritual vitiated by no base thoughts of nutrition... 'A cup of tea and a packet of assorted biscuits.' Twopence the tea, twopence the biscuits, a perfectly balanced meal.

Murphy

Samuel Barclay Beckett was always rather thin. His tall, gaunt appearance, with the hawk-like head and gull's eyes, never seemed to change over the years, looks that in his younger days were reputedly devastating to women. He was a marvellous athlete when an undergraduate at Trinity College Dublin but, apparently, was not at all interested in food. His mother (with whom he had a prickly relationship) used to journey into town from the upper-middle-class suburb of Foxrock with hampers of goodies to sustain him, and an acute curiosity about his activities. Missed meals did not preclude success in golf, boxing and cricket; Beckett is the only Nobel prize winner to appear in Wisden's *Cricketers' Almanack*. His obituary is included in the 1990 Almanack; the only other writer of note to have appeared was PG Wodehouse. In *More Pricks Than Kicks* (1934) Belacqua, the benighted student lover, takes two and a half pages to make two slices of burnt toast which he then spreads with salt, mustard and cayenne pepper (butter is for wimps such as Senior Fellows and Salvationists). He then makes his diurnal trip to the family grocer where the daily slice of gorgonzola awaits. So does bitter disappointment:

He stooped and smelt it. A faint fragrance of corruption. What good was that? He didn't want fragrance, he wasn't a bloody gourmet, he wanted a good stench.

The grocer is distressed but puts up a good defence:

'In the length and breadth of Dublin', said the grocer, 'you won't find a rottener bit this minute'.

Belacqua ate his grotesque lunch (the cheese fortunately proving rottener than at first sniff) in his favourite pub, but his day was not to improve, and if you do not wish to be deterred from eating lobster do not read of its execution at the end of the chapter.

The consumption of food in Beckett's desolate but blackly comic world is an experience imbued with danger. When Krapp opens his second drawer to liberate a large banana and then moves (Beckett's stage directions are always precise) stage front, peels it, drops the skin at his feet and begins to eat it, we expect the inevitable 'man slips on banana skin' routine. He does.

In *Molloy* the apparently uncomplicated action of the handing over of a cup of tea becomes an occasion of premonitory peril:

She was holding out to me, on an odd saucer, a mug full of a greyish concoction which must have been green tea with saccharine and powdered milk. Nor was that all, for between mug and saucer a thick slab of dry bread was precariously lodged, so that I began to say, in a kind of anguish, It's going to fall, it's going to fall, ... as if it mattered whether it fell or not.

The Beckettian landscape became increasingly bare and empty over the decades; death, the only proper theme, and suffering, the only reality. But the indomitable quality of the human creature always wins out. We laugh 'astride the grave' and the laughter redeems us. If there's no food there are always pebbles.

A little pebble in your mouth, round and smooth, appeases, soothes, makes you forget your hunger, forget your thirst.

The characters that populate Irish novels seem to spend a great deal of time drinking tea. Beckett's work is no exception, 'A nice cup of tea, drink it before it coagulates'.

Picnics, however uncomfortable, seem to have been an important feature of Irish life. The upper classes indulged on a grand scale; one thinks of Lady Gregory's lavish spreads at her house, Coole, in County Galway, or the memorable if rather disaster-prone outings described by Somerville and Ross. James Joyce and Patrick Kavanagh describe more modest expeditions, while Samuel Beckett gives us the ultimate example of what can go wrong when lunching al fresco with the wrong people in *Malone Dies*.

Lady Pedal's boating picnic develops into a blood bath as Ernest carries the hamper onto the island and is hatcheted to death, fast followed by poor Maurice. Then Lady Pedal, charmingly calling the sailors to their tea before it gets cold, is also similarly dispatched, a tiny sandwich clutched in her old hand.

Beckett's vision of the end, the undiscovered country, has strong culinary undertones:

> *Sky earth the whole kit and Boodle. Not another crumb of carrion left. Lick chops and basta.*

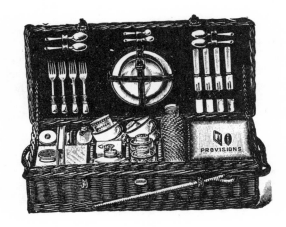

TUNA OMELETTE

no appetite a crumb of tunny then mouldy eat mouldy no need to
worry I won't die I'll never die of hunger

How It Is

The thought of a tuna omelette might not immediately appeal but it's well worth a
try because it's surprisingly delicious. In France it's known as a 'Curé's omelette' —
a happy Beckettian association as 'Curé' is one of the devastating insults
(culminating in 'Critic'!) exchanged by Vladimir and Estragon in *Waiting for
Godot.*

In *How It Is* the narrator travels horizontally through mud on an unspeakable
journey, dragging a sack of tins. Finding the tin-opener is problematic in this
condition, but without it he starves; don't suppose he could make an omelette
either.

> 1oz (30g) butter
> 1 leek or 2 scallions (spring onions)
> ½ clove of garlic
> 4 eggs
> 1 tbsp water
> black pepper
> pinch of salt
> chopped parsley
> 4oz (120g) tinned tuna

Melt the butter in the frying pan until very hot, add the finely chopped leek or
scallions and crushed garlic, and cook until soft.

Beat the 4 eggs thoroughly and add the water, lots of black pepper and a pinch
of salt. Put chopped parsley into the pan and then pour on the egg mix — the heat
should be fairly high as omelettes are cooked quickly. Cook slightly by tipping the
pan, allowing the egg to cover the surface. Add the chopped tuna. Lift the side of
the omelette gently until the mixture is set. Fold and serve with fresh bread and a
tomato salad.

Serves two.

IRISH STEW

I peered into the pots. Irish stew. A nourishing and economical dish, if a little indigestible. All honour to the land it has brought before the world.

Molloy

Clodagh King lives on Achill Island in County Mayo. She is an amazing cook and hostess and always looks impeccably glamorous despite the prevailing winds in that corner of Ireland. Heinrich Böll describes her in his *Irish Journal* as the doctor's wife with the pearly pink fingernails running a practice at the edge of Europe. Her recipe for Irish Stew is unrivalled, so we make no apologies for including Irish Stew, even though it is a common feature in all Irish cookbooks.

8 gigot lamb chops
$3^1/2$ pt ($1^3/4$l) water
salt and black pepper
2 bay leaves
2 sprigs thyme
2 sage leaves
2 sprigs parsley
4 large carrots
4 parsnips
1 large turnip
4 large onions
about 12 medium potatoes

Place the chops in a very large saucepan, add the water and season with salt and pepper. Tie the herbs in a bouquet garni and place in the saucepan. Bring to the boil very gently, then simmer while you prepare the vegetables. Chop the vegetables and cut the potatoes into halves. Put a layer of onions on top of the meat, then a layer of carrots, followed by the turnips and parsnips. Season each layer to taste. The top layer should be potatoes. Bring back to the boil and simmer gently for $1^1/2$ to 2 hours. This amount serves four ravenous or eight normal people.

ASSASSINATION CUSTARD

What's that?
A little green fry or a mushroomy one?
Two lashed ovaries with prosticiutto.

Whoroscope

When Samuel Beckett went to Paris in 1930 he discovered his true home, a place of liberation in both the personal and professional sense. He became a member of James Joyce's inner circle, and was one of the many accoucheurs at the prolonged delivery of *Finnegans Wake*.

In the early hours of 7 January 1939, Beckett was returning home with friends from a café when he was accosted by a pimp called Prudent. When Beckett repelled the pimp's advances he stuck a flick knife straight into Beckett's chest, missing the heart by a mere whisker. His companions roared for help and were assisted by a passing piano student, Suzanne Deschevaux-Dumesnil, and Beckett was rushed to hospital. Joyce insisted on paying for a private room for him, and lent him his favourite reading lamp. Nora made one of her special custard puddings to nourish the invalid. The cool and efficient piano student eventually became Mrs Beckett.

> 5 egg yolks
> 1oz (30g) castor sugar
> 1 pt (600ml) single cream
> 2 tbsp brandy

Preheat oven to 160°C (325°F, Gas mark 3).

Grease a shallow ovenproof dish (about 900ml or 1½ pt capacity). Beat the egg yolks and castor sugar together. Heat the cream gently, do not boil, and stir in the brandy. Very gradually add the warmed cream to the egg mixture, beating constantly. Pour into the dish. Place the dish in a baking tin and pour sufficient hot water into the tin to come half-way up the dish. Bake for 45 minutes or until set.
Serves four.

GOOSEBERRY FOOL

— gooseberries, she said. I said again I thought it was hopeless
and no good going on and she agreed, without opening her eyes.
Krapp's Last Tape

We really ought to have a dessert now to provide a little light relief. A gooseberry
one in memory of Krapp's lady who scratched her thighs while picking them (the
gooseberries, that is!).

    1lb (480g) fresh gooseberries
    4oz (120g) castor sugar
    ¼ pt (150ml) natural yoghurt
    ¼ pt (150ml) fresh cream

Prepare the gooseberries (top, tail and wash) and put them in a saucepan with the
sugar and a little water. Simmer gently until the gooseberries are soft. Purée the
fruit in the food processor and stir in the yoghurt. Whip the cream and fold into
the gooseberry purée. Chill for at least 2 hours before serving.
Serves four.

STICKY BUNS

Ernest, hand out the buns, said Lady Pedal.

Malone Dies

As students we spent as many hours in Bewley's Oriental Café in Grafton Street as our limited budgets allowed. The wondrous sticky buns of memory have no doubt improved with nostalgia, but the smell of freshly ground coffee wherever sniffed, still evokes an instant trip to the Dublin of the bouncy sixties. These buns are the nearest we've come across to the buns of a *Temps Perdu,* and our children love them. Move over, Proust!

Turn oven on low, so cooker top is warm and can be used to raise the dough.

> 1 tbsp honey
> $\frac{1}{4}$ pt (150ml) warm water
> $\frac{1}{2}$ pt (300ml) warm milk
> 1 level tbsp dried yeast
> 1lb (480g) plain white flour
> 1 tsp salt
> $\frac{1}{2}$ tsp each of ground cinnamon, nutmeg and allspice.
> 2oz (60g) sugar
> 6oz (180g) currants
> 2 eggs, beaten
> 3 tbsp sunflower oil

Glaze

> 1 eggwhite
> icing sugar

Mix the honey with water and milk. Sprinkle in yeast and 4 tablespoons of the flour. Mix gently and cover with a clean cloth. Leave in a warm place until frothy (20 to 25 minutes).

Sift together the flour, salt, spices and sugar, and stir into the yeast mixture. Add in the currants, eggs and oil. Mix well. If the dough is too wet, add a little more flour. Then turn out on a large wooden board with some flour and knead for approximately 10 minutes.

Scrape out the mixing bowl; put some oil in the bottom of the bowl and place the dough in upside down. Turn it around to oil it and then turn it the right way up. Leave in a warm place to rise (covered with a clean damp cloth) until double in size (about 1 hour).

Turn oven temperature up to 200°C (400°F, Gas mark 6).

Remove dough from bowl. Divide into 16 pieces, knead gently into ball shapes and brush with beaten egg yolk. Reserve the egg white for the glaze when the buns are cooked. Place the buns on oiled baking trays and bake at 200°C (400°F, Gas mark 6) for 20 to 25 minutes.

Beat 1 eggwhite until frothy and add icing sugar to taste. Brush over hot buns. Makes 16 buns.

GINGER SNAP BISCUITS

Nagg: [Holding up the biscuit] Do you want a bit?
Nell: No. (Pause.) Of what?
Nagg: Biscuit. I've kept you half. (He looks at the biscuit.
Proudly.) Three-quarters. For you. Here. (He proffers the
biscuit.) No? (Pause) Do you not feel well?

Endgame

Beckett's favourite play was not *Waiting for Godot*, which brought him fame in the early fifties, but *Endgame*, in which two of the characters, Nagg and Nell, conduct a rather limited relationship from the confines of their dustbins. Playing Nell, Veronica did her stint in the bin when at Trinity College Dublin. The scene where Nagg offers Nell three-quarters of his biscuit, accompanied by the romantic preliminary 'Time for love?', still provokes a giggle.

    12oz (360g) butter
    14oz (420g) castor sugar
    2 eggs
    ½ teacup of molasses
    1lb (480g) sifted plain flour
    2 tsp baking powder
    2 tsp ground cinnamon
    2 tsp ground cloves
    2 tsp ground ginger
    4oz (120g) granulated sugar

Preheat oven to 190°C (375°F, Gas mark 5).

Cream the butter until soft and light. Add the castor sugar and mix well. Beat in the eggs and molasses with some of the flour. Sift together the rest of the dry ingredients and mix, little by little, into the butter and sugar mixture, beating hard.

Roll about 1 teaspoon of the dough at a time into balls and then roll each ball in granulated sugar. Place on a greased baking sheet about 3 inches apart to allow for spreading and bake at 190°C (375°F, Gas mark 5) for 12 to 15 minutes. Makes about 100 biscuits, enough for two greedy people.

12

Mary Lavin

Mary Lavin, short-story writer, was born in Walpole, Massachusetts, and brought to live in Ireland by her Irish mother at the age of nine. Her first collection of short stories, *Tales from Bective Bridge*, was published in 1942. She wrote two novels, *The House on Clewe Street* and *Mary O'Grady*, and many collections of stories. She won the James Tait Memorial Prize in 1943, two Guggenheim awards and the Ellen Lynam Cabot award. Lord Dunsany, writer and big-game hunter, admired the 'astonishing insights' of her writing, which Lavin describes as 'looking closer than normal into the human heart'. Mary Lavin lives in Dublin.

Mary Lavin

b. 1912

> There was nothing Miss Lomas liked better than getting up a
> decent meal for men capable of appreciating it. Hearty food for
> hearty eaters. After she'd warned the men to mind the plates that
> were always mad hot, although never as in lesser establishments,
> disfigured by oven-marks, she would ladle out the huge helpings
> of prime beef cooked to a nicety and plentifully doused with
> gravy from the pan-liquor.
>
> 'The Mock Auction' from *In the Middle of the Fields*

'I was a great cook and I love food but I don't know whether there's any food in my books.' Mary Lavin loves food, or, more accurately, she loves good food, believing that a taste for excellence was encouraged by the many dinners she attended at embassies, universities and hotels during her distinguished career as Ireland's most eminent short-story writer, a position she has held for over forty years.

Her genius as a writer lies in her extraordinary empathy with her characters. She has an unerring, intuitive knack of cutting straight to the quick and laying bear the interior truth of ordinary lives. It is her belief 'in the power of imagination to arrive at truth' that inspires her stories, which are sometimes achingly funny, sometimes sad, and always memorable. It is not difficult to become a Lavin addict. She deals with the universal themes of love and death, loss and loneliness, freedom and betrayal, but always within the framework of ordinary things, ordinary days, ordinary people.

To counter Mary Lavin's doubt about the occurrence of food in her stories, one could say that just as her characters fall in love and have babies and work and die, so do they eat breakfast, lunch and dinner, and, as in so much of Irish literature and Irish life, drink copious amounts of tea!

> *When Kate went out, Ros took down the tea-caddy from the dresser and put*
> *a few pinches of tea from it into an earthenware pot on the hob of the big*
> *open fire. Then, taking the kettle that hung from a crane over the flames, she*
> *wet the tea, and pouring out a cup she carried it over to the window and set*
> *it to cool on the sill...*

But Mary Lavin only describes meals in detail for a specific purpose. Lord Dunsany, writer and fellow Meath-person, with a most bizarre style in hand-writing, wrote in his introduction to her first collection *Tales from Bective Bridge*: 'I do not think one finds Mary Lavin ever wasting a word.'

Nor does she waste metaphor or image; where food is described in detail it is for a good reason.

Thus in 'The Becker Wives' the dinner is described in exaggerated terms and increasing pace as the meal becomes a race and every course a hurdle:

> *The fish however had gone the way of the soup and still there was no sign of Theobald, and soon the dinner was mid-way through courses, or at least mid-way through its courses with regard to the number of dishes that had been consumed, although considering the nature of the courses, it might be said that the dinner was near its end, or rather that having successfully crossed the biggest of the fences, the guests were coming into the straight, and would gather speed now for the gallop home. In other words, having consumed the turtle soup, the curled whiting, the crown roast of young beef, accompanied by mounds of mashed potatoes, and little heaps of brussels sprouts, they might be expected to make quicker progress through the following and lighter dishes, the green salad and the peach melba, the sliver of anchovy on toast, the cheese crackers, the coffee and the crème de menthe.*

An integral part of Mary Lavin's vision is a blackly comic vein, the humour of the gallows, the humour that inspires the incident in *The House in Clewe Street* where two funeral processions take part in a grisly race to the graveyard. And food can become a comic device. In 'A Pure Accident' a deranged priest visits an old lady in hospital whom he had accidentally assaulted in his darkened church. During the visit lunch is served. The priest smells the soup curiously and asks the ward maid to tell him what it is.

> *'Cocky-leaky, Father,' she said.*
> *Instantly the priest let go the spoon, which fell back into the soup-plate, splashing the soup over the sheets.*
> *'That's enough out of you!' he cried. And catching the girl by the arm he pushed her out of the room. 'Did you hear that?' he demanded of Annie. 'You'd think butter wouldn't melt in her mouth, and then she comes out with that smut. Oh, I know her kind. And I know how I drew the smut down on me. It was mentioning her ugly stumps of legs that did it.'*

But the shock that the innocent ward maid and the soup gives him precipitates the climax of the story, a confrontation with nature, a suggestion of future freedom.

Vera is the heroine of 'Villa Violetta', a tale of a writing widow with three daughters visiting Italy with the help of a literary grant, in the hope that the Italian experience will heal their sadness and dislodge her writer's block. But the anxieties caused by accommodation problems, budgeting and naughty children preclude any creative activity until the family ends up in a convent run as a guesthouse by Irish nuns; nuns who will have nothing to do with pernicious foreign cooking — not so much ante-pasta as anti-pasta:

'We had a very good lunch.'
The nun turned and stared blankly at her.
'That's something unusual in Italy, isn't it?'
She then said blandly, and she glanced at the children.
'They look well though. Poor mites, the change of food is harder on them than on us.' She nodded sagaciously, '— all the old sauces, and that dirty olive oil in everything. Here in Villa Violetta we never use olive oil. As for garlic—'

The children are given rashers and eggs for their supper; children who just happen to adore spaghetti.

In the Italian stories, Mary Lavin seems to be more expansive on the subject of food, and a sensuousness creeps into her treatment of it. The priest in 'Villa Violetta' plays the counterpoint to the nun's entrenched xenophobia. He organises a coach trip for his Camden Town parishioners and arranges visits to four-star restaurants on the way. By staying with the nuns they can afford the gastronomic blow-outs which are highlights of the trip.

'Irish stew, tonight. See what I mean? I'm really sorry you weren't in Sienna with us. We had the famous Sienna dish Buristo Suino — do you know it? — it's lean pork cooked with all sorts of nuts and raisins and chunks of fat, and it has a strange piney flavour — and of course the wine was the local Brolio.'

The priest's love of food, wine and people, spills over to warm and comfort Vera, and he is the one who organises a hotel for her, an idyllic spot where the food is superb. The reader is made to feel that Vera will write again and that the children will be happy.

Mrs Traske in 'Trastavere' goes out to dinner with her daughter and a young poet and his closest friends, a married couple. The meal assumes bizarre proportions as the tensions of the eternal triangle rise to the surface.

The insufferable Della, hostess of the party and centre of the triangle, takes it upon herself to order dinner for everyone. The little fat patron offers the party the delights of his kitchen. ' "Pollo di diavolo? Saltimbocca? Abbachio alla cacciatora? Tonight it is tender...osso bucco," he whispered. "Tonight it is —." He stopped, and placing a kiss on his fat fingers, he blew it heavenward.' He then brings from the kitchen a raw steak on the palm of his hand, which Della orders for everyone. Simon suddenly rebels and changes his order to osso bucco. The tension increases during the twenty-minute wait and explodes when Della sticks her fork into his osso bucco and Simon refuses to eat it.

> *'I only wanted to see if it tasted good,' she said in a voice that for her was low and indistinct.*
> *'I don't want it,' Simon said.*
> *Stupefied they all stared.*
> *'Will you have a steak, then?' Della asked*
> *'No, I'm not hungry,' Simon said. 'You eat it if you want it.'*

Della takes on the ordering of the dessert — cheese, fruit, cassata — in her condescending manner, and the reader relishes the irony that eventually this overbearing and seemingly invulnerable woman commits suicide.

'The Long Holidays' is a marvellously funny story about Dolly, a fragile, doll-like creature 'with a tiny little figure, with its tiny feet and hands, and tiny, tiny waist'.

> *Dolly had lots of gentlemen friends. Just to look at her made gentlemen feel big and strong. But she had the same effect upon ladies; she made them feel big and strong too: and so had not many lady friends.*

Dolly marries the Major, a widower, whose ten-year-old son is due home for the summer holidays. Dolly makes treat-filled plans for the boy, but when Vinnie arrives in his hob-nailed boots, he is not quite what she expected. The crisis occurs at dinner, during the soup course, when Dolly and the Major become aware of a fetid odour, 'something dead in the woods, perhaps'. Vinnie provides the solution: 'Perhaps it's my feet that smell,' he said helpfully.

When Vinnie returns to the dining room wearing fresh socks he takes a second helping of soup and spills some. But it is in the middle of the custard and apple that Dolly notices the warts. She is so horrified and offended that she decides to take her step-son to the dispensary to have the warts removed with caustic. Vinnie tells Dolly about a boy at school who removes his class fellows' warts in exchange for getting his maths homework done; Dolly inquires about the method:

> *Vinnie looked surprised that she had to be told.*
> *'Bites them off — how else did you think?'*

Dolly exits in a rush.

In 'The Lost Child', a pregnant Renee is returning home in a taxi after being received into the Catholic Church. She recalls her husband's comment on their little son's thick hair, attributing its abundance to all the carrots she ate when pregnant. Renee disagrees; the carrots caused his sunny personality. 'Les carottes sont faire rire,' she says. The image of the carrots and the healthy mother and child are in contrast to the litter she sees on the street left by the street sellers: 'wilted and yellowing, disgusting, simply disgusting. The discarded outer leaves were trodden into the ground, rotting and beginning to give off a stench. Heads of lettuce were already a liquid mess.'

The rotting vegetation presages her impending miscarriage; its very smell a premonition of mortality.

Meals for Mary Lavin can reveal emotional states. In her novel *The House in Clewe Street* a seemingly innocent supper is in effect a sort of honey-trap for a potential suitor — plates of cold meats seductively displayed in fan-like patterns, resembling the petals of a flower, form a love feast for an unsuspecting male. Food too can be an image of hatred, which Manny discovers in 'At Sally Gap'. A gentle, ineffectual man, Manny is the object of his wife's hatred; she serves his dinner with the malevolence of true evil:

> *Manny sat down to the meal set before him on the brown paper. It was a plate of meat flanked on two sides by tallow-yellow potatoes and a mound of soggy cabbage that still held the shape of the fork with which it had been patted. Meat, potato and cabbage were all stuck fast to the plate. And around the rim of the plate, the gravy was crusted into a brown paper doily.*

As he swallows the grim stuff, he also swallows the truth about their marriage, that her disappointment in him has poisoned her mind and that she will simply hate him forever.

Mary Lavin is famous for her rare understanding of children and adolescents. Her treatment of them is full of insight and wisdom, often dealing with that first perilous move towards independence, that breaks the rules and questions the authority of priest or parent or teacher. Thus poor hungry Katey in 'A Glimpse of Katey', remembering her uneaten supper 'and the great cake that had been cut in two halves and in which the currants and candied fruits were as numerous as ink-spots on a blotter' finds herself in confrontation with her father, which leads her to betray her mother and sisters.

The climax of the story 'Scylla and Charybdis' is supper at the Big House, the residence of the Irish Ascendancy. Pidgie, the daughter of the steward, is bright and clever and has notions of climbing beyond her social station, and by some miracle, of being accepted on equal terms by the young ladies of the house. When Miss Gloria, whom she idolises, begins to favour her, Pidgie believes that her dream is about to be realised. Her hopes are shattered by the rigid class structure of the society in which she lives, where the rule of not eating with the lower orders is sacrosanct. As Miss Gloria serves her generously with supper in the diningroom, Pidgie is in ecstasy at the prospect of eating with her goddess:

> *'There's cold lamb here, I see, and some salad. And here's some salad dressing if you like it; Oh, yes, and some hard eggs?' Absently she held Pidgie's plate and waited for her to decide, but she was quite hungry herself and her eye was running over the food. 'I'll have some of that lamb, anyway,' she said. 'Oh, good, there's beetroot! I'll have that too!'*

But after generously piling up Pidgie's plate, she adds the dessert to the same beautiful Worcester dish because it will be easier to carry. Pidgie is just beginning to understand the implications of this when Miss Gloria opens the door for her and 'the next minute Pidgie and the plate were outside in the dark hall'.

Pidgie somehow survives her moment of crisis. Her disappointment, however awful, does not completely annihilate her spirit, for the next morning, when the young ladies appear on the terrace, a face peers through the laurel-leaves and 'Pidgie's little pink tongue was stuck out at them: as far as it would go'.

'A Marriage' and 'A Memory' again are based on the examination of an unequal relationship, but are written from opposing angles. In both stories, the women are deeply hurt by selfish men, and in both the men die. There exists in 'A Marriage' an extraordinary description of globe artichokes, and it is no surprise to discover that Mary Lavin loved growing vegetables. She grew every vegetable that it was possible to grow in Ireland; her aubergines were famous. She says that in the Bective Bridge days her life was composed of writing and gardening. She has great sympathy with the character of the gardener in the story 'The New Gardener', as he tips out the bag of delicious cream buns and says:

'No matter. Food comes first. Learn to distinguish.'

SCALLOPS IN WHITE WINE SAUCE

Nicely browned, a delicious cheesy smelling sauce bubbled and winked around the brink of an earthenware pan. 'Not scallops?' she exclaimed, appreciatively licking her lips. 'I meant them to be a surprise. I know you love them.'

'A Walk on the Cliff' from *A Family Likeness*

Veronica loves seafood, and this is her favourite way of doing scallops. It can work as a starter or a main course and is so visually pleasing because of the scallop shells.

        1 doz medium size scallops
        1 1/2oz (45g) butter
        1 1/2 oz (45g) flour
        1/2 pt (300ml) milk
        1/4pt (150ml) fish stock
        pepper and salt
        3 tbsp dry white wine
        2 tbsp fresh cream
        2oz (60g) white breadcrumbs
        1 lemon
        parsley to garnish

Poach scallops in stock for 5 minutes. Remove, and place in shells.

Make sauce by melting butter, add flour and stir. Add milk and fish stock slowly and cook for a further 5 to 7 minutes, stirring constantly. Add seasoning, wine and cream and pour over scallops in shells. Sprinkle with breadcrumbs and dot with a little butter. Place under a hot grill for a few minutes until the tops are golden brown. Serve garnished with lemon and parsley.
Serves four.

MACKEREL WITH PRUNE STUFFING

Mackerel is not a very popular fish, he explained to Maud, 'It's
regarded as a scavenger. Fresh out of the sea, though, and properly
cooked, the way Veronica does it, can be delicious. We have
developed a real passion for it.'

'A Walk on the Cliff' from *A Family Likeness*

We're not certain how Mary Lavin's Veronica cooks mackerel, but this Veronica
simply throws fresh mackerel on the frying pan with a knob of butter and turns it
over once. Fionn likes to serve it with stewed gooseberries or rhubarb; the sharpness
of the fruit goes well with the oiliness of the fish.

    4 filleted mackerel
    10 prunes
    4oz (120g) long grain rice
    2 oz (60g) melted butter
    salt and pepper
    4 tomatoes
    parsley to garnish

Preheat oven to 200°C (400°F, Gas mark 6).

Rinse and dry the mackerel. Soak prunes, preferably overnight, in strained tea, or
for at least 5 hours. Stone and chop the prunes. Cook rice in lightly salted boiling
water. This will take 10 to 15 minutes. Drain the rice and add the prunes and
melted butter or margarine. Season with salt and pepper. Divide stuffing between
the 4 fillets; fold fillets over to enclose stuffing. Place in greased casserole, cover and
bake for approximately 30 minutes. Serve immediately, garnished with tomato and
parsley.
Serves four.

ARTICHOKE BOTTOMS WITH ASPARAGUS TIPS À L'ESTRAGON

> On her arm she had a garden trug filled with globe artichokes which she held up to show him. 'Did you ever see anything as perfect, James? Such a blend of purple and green. They're a different variety from the all-green ones we have been growing. They are supposed to be more succulent. They're certainly exquisite looking, aren't they? They remind me of those porcelain ones we went so near to buying in Paris.'
>
> 'A Marriage' from *A Family Likeness*

When the children were little our two families used to go on holidays to France and stay in *gîtes* in lovely places like the Loire Valley and the Dordogne. We all loved visits to the *supermarché*, where everything seemed more interesting than at home. Some of us frequented the *charcuterie* and nobody turned down a visit to the *patisserie* — the very thought of the strawberry tarts brings tears to the eyes. We always returned to Ireland laden with jars of asparagus and jam, bottles of wine, *fonds d'artichaux*, cheese and pâté. Artichokes always make us think of those good times, when we all ate far too much and didn't care a bit.

1 340g tin asparagus
1 400g jar artichoke bottoms
5 tbsp cream
2 oz (60g) butter
4 egg yolks
salt and pepper
2 tbsp tarragon vinegar
a little chopped tarragon

Heat the asparagus and the artichoke bottoms. Place on a warmed dish.

Put the cream, butter, eggs, salt and pepper in a bowl and place it over a pot of boiling water. Stir until the sauce begins to thicken. Then add the vinegar and the tarragon and pour it over the artichokes.

This may seem a rather rich sauce but it is delicious and goes extremely well with the earthy flavours of the artichokes and asparagus, which for real luxury ought to be fresh.

Serves four.

PHEASANT STEW

'Last Sunday, I saw a pheasant', she said. 'On your own land?' he asked eagerly. 'A hen?' 'I think so. Yes, it was a hen, of course — the duller of the two, isn't it?' 'I should think so!' he said.

'The Lucky Pair' from *In the Middle of the Fields*

One no longer needs a gunman in the family, or even the shadow of one, as pheasant has become a common sight in the shops during the winter, and is quite reasonably priced.

Fionn does a wonderful winter dinner party which stars several brace of pheasant in the leading role. Sometimes she roasts them in half a pint of red wine, with streaky rashers draped over the breasts to keep them moist for about 1 hour at oven heat 190°C to 200°C (400°F, Gas mark 6).

Fionn also makes this pheasant stew. Both pheasant dishes are good with roast potatoes and red cabbage.

2 pheasants
½ tsp powdered ginger
salt and pepper
3oz (90g) butter
2 onions, chopped
1 tsp each turmeric and ground cumin
juice of 1 lemon
wine-glass of sherry
1 tsp Marmite
1 395g tin chopped tomatoes
1 tsp Worcestershire sauce

Joint the bird and season it with ginger, salt and pepper. Fry gently in a heavy pot with the butter and onions. Cover, and cook slowly for 20 minutes. Then add the turmeric, cumin, lemon juice, sherry, Marmite, tomatoes and Worchestershire sauce. Simmer for 30 minutes. Serve with rice, button mushrooms and tiny tomatoes.
Serves four.

SHEPHERD'S PIE

'Some cats have to put up with a steady diet of Shepherd's Pie and meat loaf.'
They were inside now, and he sank down on the sofa. Myra, who was still standing, shuddered.
'What would I do if you were the kind of man who did like shepherd's pie?' she said. 'I'm sure there are such men.' But she couldn't keep up the silly chaff. 'I think maybe I'd love you enough to try and make it —' she laughed, ' — if I could.'
'A Memory' from *A Memory and Other Stories*

If real men don't eat quiche, what sort of men eat shepherd's pie? And do real cats eat meat loaf? Enough of the metaphysics; at the risk of proposing something that Myra would find naff, we think shepherd's pie and its sibling, cottage pie, are excellent fodder for hungry families. This shepherd's pie is Fionn's recipe. Of course, if you're fresh out of shepherds....

2 onions, chopped
4 cloves garlic, chopped
4 tbsp sunflower oil
1lb (480g) lean beef, minced
3 heaped tbsp cornflour
½ pt (300ml) beef stock
¼ pt (150ml) leftover wine (optional)
2 tbsp tomato purée
½ tsp Marmite
salt and pepper
½lb (240g) peas
½lb (240g) carrots, sliced
3lb (1½k) boiled potatoes, mashed with ½ pt (300ml) milk and 2oz (60g) butter

Preheat oven to 175°C, 350°F, Gas mark 4.

Fry the onions and garlic in the oil until soft. Add the meat and stir till browned. Mix the cornflour with half the stock, then mix in the wine, the rest of the stock, the tomato purée and the Marmite. Pour this over the meat. Season well, cover, and simmer for 10 minutes, then pour it all into an oven-proof dish. Stir in the vegetables and top with the mashed potato. Bake for one hour.
Serves four.

LEMON BLANCMANGE

> Hastily putting down her own plate, she picked up a silver spoon and pointed to the top shelf of the sideboard where, unnoticed by Pidgie, there were bowls of jelly and bowls of prunes and a great big dish of pink blancmange with only a small helping taken from it.
>
> 'Scylla and Charybdis' from *The Patriot Son*

Blancmange has a fearful reputation which is based, as far as we can see, on the cornflour version; it is rather similar to wallpaper paste which has been allowed to set to a nice rubbery consistency. Victorian recipes use isinglass, a very pure form of gelatine, obtained from the air-bladders of some freshwater fish, usually the sturgeon. We have found it more convenient to use commercial gelatine than enquiring if there is a sturgeon in the house.

> 1 packet lemon jelly
> ³/₄ pt (450ml) hot water
> 2oz (60g) almond flakes
> 1 pt (600ml) cream
> 4oz (120g) castor sugar
> ¹/₂ lemon peel, finely grated
> ¹/₄ tsp cinnamon
> 5g sachet powdered gelatine
> ¹/₂ cup hot water
> 2 tbsp sweet sherry

Dissolve the lemon jelly in ³/₄ pint of hot water. Cool and leave aside until just setting. Place a mould or pudding basin in a bowl of ice cubes. Line the mould by pouring the jelly in slowly. Sprinkle some almond flakes in the mould and add some more jelly. Set aside in the refrigerator. Heat the cream with the sugar, lemon peel and cinnamon. Stir slowly till the sugar has dissolved. Melt the gelatine in ¹/₂ cup of hot water. Add this, the rest of the almonds and the sherry to the cream. Stir, mix well, then set aside till cold and just about to set. Pour into the mould on top of the lemon jelly. Put the mould back into the fridge until completely set. To serve, dip the mould for a few seconds in a bowl of hot water and turn out on a plate.
Serves four.